Garner

Without your help, there's
no way this book would
have happened. Many thanks,
and God bless you!

THE
BIG
LIE

Uncle Stan

THE BIG LIE

DISCOVERING JOY,
HAPPINESS,
AND FREEDOM BEYOND
MATERIAL SUCCESS

Stan Sanderson

Health Communications, Inc.
Deerfield Beach, Florida

www.hcibooks.com

**Library of Congress Cataloging-in-Publication Data
is available through the Library of Congress.**

ISBN-13: 978-0-7573-0662-4
ISBN-10: 0-7573-0662-4

All "Related Thoughts" and "Pertinent Quotations" in this book are from
The New Dictionary of Thoughts, A Cyclopedia of Quotations, Standard Book
Company, 1961.

HCI, its logos and marks are trademarks of Health Communications, Inc.

Publisher: Health Communications, Inc.
       3201 S.W. 15th Street
       Deerfield Beach, FL 33442–8190

Cover book design by Andrea Perrine Brower
Interior book design and formatting by Dawn Von Strolley Grove

When you find out who you really are,
you'll find what you've been looking for!

CONTENTS

Part IV. The Seven Strategies

Part V. Starting Each Day

Part VI. Real Value of the Program

Part VII. Shared Experiences

ACKNOWLEDGMENTS

I would like to express my love and gratitude to the many people without whom the Spiritual Coach Program would never have been developed, nor this book written.

First, to my dear wife, Elizabeth, who has been at my side for over fifty years, and who both loved and supported me through my many missteps in our life journey.

Second, to my four children and their lovely families, who have shown the grace to allow their dad to lecture them on how one should lead his or her life, until he finally learned the lesson. And special thanks to my youngest son, David, for encouraging me to "follow my passion," and for his assistance in the overall development of the project. Also, I would certainly be remiss if I did not thank my eldest son, Rob, for the many hours of personal and spiritual discovery we shared together, subjecting the book to a very real and practical challenge.

I am also deeply grateful to my nephew, Garner Ransom, and

his company, Crux Design Group, for their untiring efforts and cooperation in creating all of our graphics, including the website. His collaboration and insights regarding approach and presentation were invaluable.

These acknowledgments would certainly be incomplete without an attempt to mention some of the many writers and practitioners of spiritual life who have shared their experience with me and contributed to my spiritual awakening. These include such enlightened teachers and authors as Maurice Bucke, William James, Kahlil Gibran, Emmet Fox, Carl Jung, C. S. Lewis, T. S. Eliot, Bill Wilson, Joseph Campbell, M. Scott Peck, Helen Schucman, and Maharishi Mahesh Yogi. They are no longer physically present, but their spirits and contributions live on.

My list also includes contemporary seekers, teachers, authors and scholars, such as Deepak Chopra, Wayne Dyer, Paul Ferrini, Eckhart Tolle, Charles Price, and Tom Harpur. Each one individually shines his or her light upon the path, while collectively providing a "beacon of hope."

In addition, I am indebted to Burt Harding who, through sharing his writings and satsang scripts, published by the Awareness Foundation, continues to remind me of the importance of "being" here and now!

Thanks also go to my publisher, Peter Vegso, president of Health Communications Inc., and his editorial staff, for recognizing the need to share the story of *The Big Lie* with all who are yet to find the joy, happiness, and freedom they're seeking. And finally, a very special thanks to Michele Matrisciani, my editor, whose skill and expertise guided me through the process of bringing relevance and structure to a challenging subject.

Part I
INTRODUCTION

Coach's Spiritual Awakening

I recall sitting in a restaurant one night with a very good friend, discussing the meaning of life and whether it was really worth a candle. He asked me, "What is the one thing you want in life, more than anything else?" After much thought I told him that what I really wanted more than anything else in the world was to be happy. He then asked, "Would it matter what you had if you were truly happy?" Obviously the answer was no. If you're happy, you're happy! How could it matter what you have?

Through this rather simple exchange, I finally realized that what I was *really* searching for was happiness, not career accomplishment or a bigger pile of "stuff," hoping that acquiring it would somehow make me happy. It had not done so in the past, and I had no reason to believe that it would do so in the future. What was required was that I seek happiness at its Source, and not through the acquisition of *things*.

As I reflected on both my business and

personal life, it became clear to me that I had completely bought into the notion that the extent of my future happiness would be in direct proportion to that which I was able to achieve or acquire. And I wasn't alone. Almost all of my friends and associates seemed to be operating with a similar agenda, accompanied by comparable results. It's as though our families, mentors, and life coaches all subscribed to this absolute truth, "Be successful, and you'll be happy!" It's what I now call "The Big Lie."

Shortly after this insight it was suggested to me that in order to find the *true* source of happiness, I would need to look to God *as I understood him* and turn my will and my life over to his care. However, the problem with that was I didn't know what either my *will* or my *life* were really all about, nor did I have any *workable* understanding of God. And it was not at all clear to me just exactly how developing a closer relationship with him would provide the happiness I sought. Obviously, some very specific inquiries needed to be made.

This was made all the more difficult because, although I was brought up in a Christian environment, and therefore my early exposure was toward Jesus and the principles attributed to him, I tended to stay clear of anything that "smacked" of religion. I didn't see myself going to Africa to save natives, or handing out pamphlets on street corners. I saw myself more as a gentleman of leisure, driving to Florida in a convertible with the top down, a pretty woman by my side, and my golf clubs in the trunk. I believed that God took care of Heaven, and I took care of everything down here!

It wasn't long before my search for an understanding of God led me to a life-changing discovery: that there was a Power greater than myself at work in the universe, and that experiencing the joy, happiness, and freedom with which I had been endowed from the very beginning was contingent *only* upon *awakening* to my spiritual reality.

This, in turn, led me to study the techniques of Transcendental Meditation, as taught by Maharishi Mahesh Yogi, through the International Meditation Society. Soon after beginning the practice of meditation, I experienced a wonderful calming effect in both my demeanor and in my physical well-being. I seemed to intuitively know what to do in situations that used to baffle me, and my whole attitude and outlook on life changed for the better. It was truly remarkable!

I was also blessed to have discovered a book entitled *A Course in Miracles*, published by the Foundation for Inner Peace, which confirmed my personal experience and helped to inform my universal spiritual principles. It teaches that we are all interconnected as one, yet we see ourselves as separated individuals, living life through our own *perception*, rather than in the *reality* given to us directly from God. Its principal thesis is that we are all the sons of God, our mission is happiness, our function is forgiveness, and *our inheritance is joy and peace*. It's a message that speaks to my heart, and I've fully embraced these principles in my daily living.

More recently, I had the opportunity to read Deepak

Chopra's book *How to Know God*. It's a remarkable presentation of how we can actually experience the *reality* of God, rather than simply know *about* him. There is no question in my mind that Deepak's mission is to remind us that the spiritual truths of earlier times are equally true today, and that they will always be true. He does this through blending our spiritual reality with contemporary scientific understanding, in a way that confirms the omnipresence, omnipotence, and omniscience of God in our everyday life.

Perhaps the single most important function that the God of my understanding is charged with is allowing me to *experience* the joy, happiness, and freedom that he endowed me with in the beginning. Our "arrangement" in every situation is that I'm in charge of *inputs* and he's in charge of *outcomes*. I know that he goes before me and prepares the way, and that he can open "doors" I don't even know are there. It only remains for me to follow in faith and to do the best that I can with what I have, with whatever he puts in front of me. And as long as I continue to enjoy the fullness of my endowment, he controls the game!

Today, I am blessed with the "knowing-feeling" of joy, happiness, and freedom in all that I do, regardless of the situation in which I find myself. I know who I am, where I came from, and where I'm going. I now enjoy the inner peace and sense of personal fulfillment that before had been so elusive. I feel as though I'm standing on a rock, comfortable in the presence of all others, and confident in the knowledge that I belong. I have the love of my wife and family and the respect of my friends and colleagues. I enjoy perfect health, and when I put my head down at night, I sleep soundly.

There is absolutely no question in my mind that what I've experienced through my search for happiness is what is called a "spiritual awakening." I have awakened from what I think is best described as a "sleep," in which my life was being lived through my ego-self, directed by my *conditioned mind,* responding to everything that I perceived as happening in my world. It's not a complete awakening, as I believe when that happens I will be moving on from my human existence. However, what I have feels great! It fills my life with joy, happiness, and freedom. And since I've always been a pleasure seeker, and my awakening brings me so much pleasure every day, I'll continue to do the best I can with whatever God puts in front of me and accept the resulting outcome. He has never let me down, and his remarkable capabilities never cease to amaze me!

It is my sincerest wish that you too enjoy these blessings. If you already do, you know just how incredible they are, and you should continue doing whatever it is that you're doing. If you don't, then change *something.* And if you're not sure what to change, I encourage you to define the God of your personal understanding, and to let him help you discover who you really are. *For just as soon as you find out who you really are, you'll find what you've been looking for!* The Spiritual Coach Program was created specifically to help you with that discovery.

The program consists of seven concepts and seven strategies that together provide a road map for an incredible spiritual journey. The journey begins with the recognition of the Big Lie (that career and material success will bring the happiness we seek) and then leads us toward the joy of living "The 200 Percent Life" (combining 100 percent of our material world with 100 percent of our spiritual awareness).

The Spiritual Coach Program has been in development for over thirty-five years and was devised from the experience gained through personal encounters, and from the contributions of both thoughts and experiences of others who have traveled the same path. The sole criteria for the ideas shared in this book are what works and what is transferable to, and repeatable by, others in similar circumstances.

While not a religious program, I do thank the God of my understanding for making provision in his master plan for me to come to know who I really am and allowing me to discover the joy, happiness, and freedom that lie beyond material success.

God, Religion, and Gender

God is *not* religion! And religion isn't necessary for spiritual awareness. Ironically, it is often the very thing that impedes personal spiritual experience. As God does not follow any one religion, he welcomes all religions, or none.

When the word "God" is used throughout the Spiritual Coach Program, the reference is to the Prime Source, First Cause, or Whatever/Whoever is deemed to be the Creator of all things (see the glossary of terms at the end of the book). It is not meant to be associated with any particular form of organized religion. As a matter of fact, the second concept of the program requires that each participant define and choose the God of his or her *own* understanding.

The program tends to emphasize universal spiritual themes rather than religious doctrine or theory. However, since I was born into a Christian environment, it follows that many of the expressions I use are taken from Christian teachings. Such expressions are thought to be universal in concept and resonate with any and all religious teachings that espouse a similar experience. It is my belief that the substance of the stories ascribed to Horus, Jesus, Moses, Mohammed, Krishna, and Buddha (to mention only a few of the great icons and teachers) was informed by the same *reality*. It would add nothing to this program to try to rationalize the differences, definitions, or religious interpretations of competing beliefs; we must simply accept the universality of the spiritual ideas being expressed. *They all lead to God in the end!*

Most historical spiritual and religious writings refer to God in the male gender (he, him, his, and son). While it is clear to me that the magnitude of God is inclusive of, and greatly transcends, all gender considerations, the program uses the historical male reference throughout. I hope and trust that readers and participants will allow this traditional adherence in the spirit of simplicity in the presentation.

You will also notice that I often use the corporate "we" throughout the text of the Spiritual Coach Program rather than personal pronouns. This more accurately reflects the contributions of both thoughts and experiences shared with me by others who have traveled the same path.

Part II

THE SPIRITUAL COACH PROGRAM

Spiritual Coaching

On his deathbed, Buddha begged his disciples, "Do not accept what you hear by report; do not accept tradition; do not accept a statement because it is found in our books, nor because it is in accord with your belief, nor because it is the saying of your teacher. Be lamps unto yourselves."

What an absolutely perfect segue into the concept and practice of spiritual coaching. It not only takes the focus off the coach, but it makes clear wherein the responsibility for personal achievement lies. There is nothing that the most singularly skilled coach, practicing all of the discipline at his command, can do for someone that will transcend what he or she will not do for himself or herself.

Many things happen when we look to a coach for guidance, but the five most important are: (1) we take ourselves more seriously; (2) we take more efficient and focused actions immediately; (3) we stop putting up with what's dragging us down; (4) we create momentum, so it's easier to get results; and

(5) we set more focused goals than we might have without a coach. We engage a spiritual coach because we want to experience joy, happiness, and freedom in our daily lives; we want inner peace and fulfillment; and we want the path clearly defined. It's as simple as that. A spiritual coach helps us achieve all of these life goals more quickly.

The major differences between a priest, a guru, and a spiritual coach are aptly described using the metaphor of relearning to ride a bicycle after a particularly bad fall. A priest would point out your sin in causing the fall, have you atone for your sin by washing the bike once a week, and pray that you would be allowed to ride the bike again in the hereafter. The guru would help you to understand that the fall never really happened, the bike is nothing, you are nothing, everything that *is* is nothing, and that there is no need to do anything to enjoy the fullness of *being* with the bike in the here and now. The spiritual coach simply tells you to get on the bike, runs along beside you until you're well under way, and then you don't need him anymore.

As Deepak Chopra said in *How to Know God*, "The ultimate promise of Spirituality is to become the author of your own existence." This is not unlike what Buddha said to his disciples.

Objectives of the Program

A familiar saying in Buddhism is "There are many gates to the Garden [of enlightenment], but the gates are *not* the Garden" (emphasis mine). For Christians, "the Garden" is a metaphor for what the new testament refers to as "the kingdom of God." In its teaching we are counseled to "seek first the kingdom of God and His righteousness, and all these things shall be added to you" (Matthew 6:33, New King James Version; all biblical quotations are from this version).

This begs the question, "All *what* things?" The reference is to the provision of everything that we will ever need. The list, in its entirety, is descriptive of the provision, protection, and perfection that God conferred on each and every one of us in our *reality* as his creation. Of particular interest to us are the blessings of joy, happiness, and freedom, the fruits of which have been noticeably missing from what could be termed, an "otherwise successful life." Fortunately for us, these blessings can't be separated out from the others. It's a "package deal." So in finding out who we really are, we'll not only find joy, happiness, and freedom, but we'll also uncover a host of other blessings that were meant for our continued enjoyment.

The Spiritual Coach Program is *just another gate*. You only need this program if you are not yet in the Garden and you wish to enter through *this* gate. The program will be most helpful for otherwise successful people who share the additional burden expressed in the proverb, "It is easier for a camel to go through the eye of a needle than for a rich man to enter the kingdom of God" (Matthew 19:24). The reference is to someone who persists in seeking the "kingdom" through acquired wealth, powered by his or her own abilities and personal resources.

The bad news is that trying to attain "the kingdom" in this fashion is not going to happen! The good news, which many have discovered, is that with God there are no degrees of difficulty. It is equally possible for both the rich man and the poor man to enter the kingdom. The operative phrase is "with God." Once this is understood, the objective becomes crystal clear. Define the God of your personal understanding and let him help you to discover who you *really* are. With that discovery, the gate will "open" and you'll have found what you've been looking for!

How It Works

The Spiritual Coach Program is a simple program consisting of seven concepts and seven strategies that when approached as a spiritual journey allow otherwise successful people to discover the joy, happiness, and freedom that lie *beyond* material success. It assumes that each individual is committed to the objective and is willing to accept some fundamental changes in his or her approach to everyday life.

The choice of using concepts as the vehicle to briefly outline the scope of each principle is deliberate. It allows the subject to be addressed in a *directional* way, without attempting to provide all of the answers. Experience has shown that even when the objective is the same, we do not all seek with the same level of detail or intensity. It is therefore left to each participant to explore the particular concept in whatever way best suits his or her personal approach.

Before any progress can be made in solving a *perceived* problem, we must first identify the problem and determine its relative significance in our lives. The first concept in the program requires that we acknowledge and accept the fact that sustainable joy, happiness, and freedom are *not* by-products of either career accomplishment or the acquisition of anything. Our expectation that they are either one is the key factor in our continued disappointment.

Once we're clear on the fundamental source of our problem, we must reassess our previous strategy and explore alternative courses of action. This eventually, and understandably, leads us to the consideration of God. In the second concept, we define our God and determine the extent of his capabilities. Our insistence is that he is able to deliver the joy, happiness, and freedom we seek. We must be sure to empower him in accordance with our needs, as he can only accomplish that which we will *allow* him to do!

Immediately upon defining and choosing our God, we put him to work on our behalf. The third concept requires that we make a decision to allow him to take the lead role in our lives. This is not an easy task, but one of paramount importance if progress is to be made. We see the problem. There is a solution. Now is the time to change direction. Engaging God's awesome power to accomplish our objectives is an exciting prospect!

The fourth concept requires that we review our behavior patterns and past performances to find out what really makes us "tick." We look at ourselves objectively, perhaps for the first time, and allow ourselves to make new decisions about future actions. It's remarkable how good it makes us feel to have spent the time and to have made the effort to "clean house."

Just as the fourth concept allows us to discover any number of personal behavior problems or situations in need of correction, the fifth concept presents us with an opportunity to make any reparations that may be necessary. We also come to know that by forgiving the mistakes of others, we too are forgiven. Once this process is completed, we sense the lifting of a tremendous weight from our shoulders and begin to experience what freedom really feels like!

The sixth concept allows us to establish conscious contact with God through the use of prayer and meditation. These communication techniques are essential to discovering our true potential, and to experiencing successful outcomes in all that we do, with effortless ease. God seems to go before us to prepare the way, and opens "doors" that we didn't even know were there.

And finally, having been thorough in our approach to the preceding concepts, the seventh concept confirms our ability to enjoy both our material success and the joy, happiness, and freedom discovered through awareness of our spiritual reality. We recognize that God is doing for us what we were unable to do for ourselves.

It is suggested that you work through the concepts in numerical order, using the seven strategies to assist you in personalizing the process. The program is not meant to be learned by rote and discussed intellectually. It is *experiential* in nature, with progress made in one concept leading to a better appreciation and readiness to experience the next, and so on. Each participant proceeds at his or her own pace. You'll come to recognize that the objective is not to *finish* the program, but rather to *awaken* to your spiritual reality while savoring the fruits of the journey.

To assist your journey even further, "Coach's Messages" are included throughout the book to help change the internal dialogue associated with the Big Lie. Our all-too-human reasoning process, or conditioned responses to everyday situations, can lead us to fall deeper into the seduction of career and material success, so the Coach's Messages were designed to help develop new perceptions of success and provide alternative approaches for implementing these into our lives. Let's face it, we've lived a long time buying into the false promises of the Big Lie, and old habits die hard. Each Coach's Message will provide new insights, thereby challenging stereotypical thoughts and conditioned responses and helping you redefine success as you know it.

After starting the program, you are encouraged to immediately begin applying and practicing your newly acquired insights in your daily activities. Subsequently, through continued practice of the program, you'll discover the joy, happiness, and freedom that lie beyond material success, and you'll make a quantum leap in your enjoyment of life.

Part III

THE SEVEN CONCEPTS

First Concept: The Big Lie

The real goal of anyone pursuing career and material success is to experience the joy, happiness, and freedom these successes promise to bring to his or her daily life. Almost all of us have bought into the idea that a successful career and the acquisition of things will allow us to live happily ever after.

The problem is that it doesn't work. It never has, and it never will. It's what we call, "The Big Lie." The reason it doesn't work, quite simply, is that happiness is not a by-product of the *acquisition* of anything. It therefore follows that no level of business or career accomplishment (no matter how grandiose the title) nor any amount of material success will bring the joy, happiness, and freedom we seek.

Belief in the Big Lie is a phenomenon experienced by most people in the developed world. We see evidence everywhere of both its presence and the devastating effect it has had on so many lives. Dramatic examples are seen in the increased number of substance abuse problems and reported suicides among the rich and famous, many of whom were thought to have *everything*, yet lived an empty existence.

Upon reflection, however, we may well feel that the poorest among us are those who do not attempt to "escape" and are simply disillusioned by the absence of fulfillment, approaching each day with a sense of boredom and futility.

Searching for happiness in the wrong places is perhaps one of our biggest mistakes. And this will not change until we discover the true nature of happiness and embrace it in our personal lives. Our "ladder" is leaning against the wrong "building." Even as we reach the top of the ladder, we're not where we want to be!

Our Creator endowed us with perfect joy, happiness, and freedom at the outset, which we have somehow forgotten. Instead of seeking to achieve personal fulfillment through acquiring an ever-increasing number of *outside* things, we need only look *inside* and discover who we really are.

There's an old saying, "If we were to run out of things to acquire, we'd have to look at ourselves!" That would certainly prevent our ego-self from playing the "seek and do not find" game; if we focus our attention on knowing who we really are, we can allow ourselves to benefit from the "seek and you shall find" promise.

A new awareness is required. To experience the joy, happiness, and freedom we seek, we must recognize this flawed strategy and decide on a new course of action.

COACH'S MESSAGE

Are You as Important and as Blessed as Anyone You Know?

I certainly hope you feel this way! When you realize that you were created by God, made perfectly in his image, blessed with all that you will ever need, both now and for eternity, and that no one was given a greater measure (or a lesser one) of anything, your *relative* importance becomes self-evident. Do you know that? Can you feel the *magnitude* of this idea?

But, you may say, what about all of the "stuff" that others have and I don't have? It certainly *looks* as though they've received a greater measure. There seems to be a clear discrepancy between what's being said and what actually happens. If that thought enters your head, as it does for most of us, you need to look very carefully at both the question and the implied conclusions.

First, the gifts given to each of us by God equally are all "ends," not "means." When God gives something, by definition it is perfect and complete and requires no enhancement. It is given once and is yours forever! Hence, the joy, happiness, and freedom given to you in the very beginning are yours to enjoy each and every moment of each and every day, both now and for eternity.

The only way you can possibly *feel* that you don't have these gifts is if you have *forgotten who you really are*. Should this happen, you'll find yourself looking to "acquire" them through outside sources. That's where "stuff" becomes important in your life. Stuff is a *means*—not an *end!* In this example you'll be looking for it to provide the feelings of joy and happiness that *seem* to be missing.

Unfortunately, it's not going to happen, no matter how much stuff you may accumulate, simply because joy and happiness are not by-products of the acquisition of anything. They are a *prescribed* gift from God, and as such are yours to enjoy always and forever! There is no one who has one iota of anything important for your joy of life that you do not also possess. The gifts you were given are "ends"—you already have them.

All that's necessary is for you to *remember* who you really are, and that when God gives you something, it's yours forever! Don't get caught up in suffering a shortfall of any kind, at any time, but rather accept whatever situation you may find yourself in and do the best you can with what you have. Then, and only then, will you experience how important you really are. Try it, and see what happens! God blesses you.

Moment of Reflection
"The Big Lie"

Underlying Principle: Awareness, *n.*, having knowledge of a situation or fact. (*Oxford Dictionary of Current English*, Third Edition)

Implicit Question: Am I aware that my "ladder," which was meant to lead me to personal fulfillment, has been leaning against the wrong "building"?

Personal Discovery: Exactly what is it that allows me to believe that additional career or material success will provide the happiness I'm seeking? Why has it not yet happened?

Related Thought: "Success is full of promise till men get it, and then it is as last year's nest, from which the bird has flown."

—H. W. Beecher (1813–1887)

Second Concept: The God Thing

Having come to the realization that happiness is not found in career or material success, we need to look elsewhere. And that *elsewhere* will eventually and understandably lead us to God. This means we are going to have to talk about "The God Thing," but perhaps in a way that you may not have previously considered.

The problem is that a high percentage of otherwise successful people have virtually no *personal* relationship with God. There seems to be a direct correlation between the pursuit of business or professional success and the *absence* of any personal relationship with God. The commitment we make to "improving" our lives through the acquisition of things doesn't allow much time for the development of such a relationship. It's not that we don't *believe*—it's just that we don't know him all that well.

Anyone can begin to develop a personal relationship with God by simply answering two questions: "Who is he?" and "What can he do for me?" As to the first question, most of us would agree that, by any definition, God would have to be all-powerful, all-knowing, and always present, in addition to being both compassionate and merciful. He would also be the Creator of all living things, including each one of us.

However, there is no spiritual requirement that any of us must accept somebody else's God as our own. We're completely free to figure out for ourselves who God is. In fact, our relationship with God, as each one of us understands him, is *personal* and has nothing to do with whomever or whatever somebody else's God may be.

As to the second question, "What can he do for me?" we are told in the New Testament of the Bible (Paul's letter to the churches of Galatia), "The fruit of the Spirit is love, joy, peace, longsuffering, kindness, goodness, faithfulness" (Galatians 5:22), which sounds a lot like what many of us are searching for! Regardless, our primary interest is that he can provide us with *sustainable* joy, happiness, and freedom each and every day of our life. This has to be the test, and this is the principal objective to which we are fully committed.

We need to undertake the "recruitment" of our own God. And, in so doing, we must make sure that he possesses all of the characteristics necessary to achieve our stated goals. No one needs God in his or her life to be miserable or to be just "fine"; we're quite capable of doing that on our own. Our invitation for God to join us will be contingent on his ability to help us discover the joy, happiness, and freedom we seek.

What Is the Atonement?

It's when we acknowledge who we *really* are. It's a term often used in spiritual discussions to properly position ourselves in the Father, Son, Holy Spirit, (Trinity) understanding of the Christian belief system (other belief systems use different names to describe similar relationships).

To accept the Atonement is to recognize that we are "at one" (atoned) with God and his kingdom and that we have been given everything we will ever need to live a life of joy, happiness, and freedom, as he willed from the very beginning.

When asked who we are, and why we're here, most of us respond by giving our name, address, and cell phone number, along with our personal story of what we've been doing since we "arrived" on this earth. And, of course, if good things have happened to us, we'll say how diligent we've been. If we've screwed up, we'll point out how it wasn't really our fault.

However, the Atonement is the answer we give if we are indeed living, or are seeking to live, lives filled with joy, happiness, and freedom, as God so ordained. It's the difference between living a "separated" life and a life that is, or wants to be, "at one" with God and all of his creation.

It helps me to remember who I really am, and where I stand

in God's kingdom, when each morning I say what I call the "Remembrance Prayer." Try it, and see what happens! God blesses you.

REMEMBRANCE PRAYER

God, I accept the Atonement.
Help me to remember that I am one with all created things;
The Son of God, and the light of the world;
The brother of Jesus, and of all people, in Christ;
And that the Holy Spirit is our Guide and Teacher.
My mission is happiness,
My function is forgiveness, and
My inheritance is joy and peace. Amen.

Moment of Reflection
"The God Thing"

Underlying Principle: Acceptance, *n.*, the act of willingly accepting something offered or proposed.

Implicit Question: Am I willing to accept the idea of a personal relationship with God?

Personal Discovery: If I were to describe my current relationship with God to a close friend, what might that sound like?

Related Thought: "The more we let God take us over, the more truly ourselves we become—because he made us."

—C. S. Lewis (1898–1963)

Third Concept: The Power Shift

Now that we have chosen our God and endowed him with some impressive attributes, what do we do with him? We put him to work! We extend an invitation to him to participate in our daily lives. Only by doing this are we able to employ all of his power toward the accomplishment of our objectives. We call this, "The Power Shift."

The problem most of us have with accepting God into our lives is that we might become too altruistic and have to give up some of our "stuff." Truthfully, a very high percentage of us have an underlying fear that to be into the God "thing" equates to denying ourselves the "good life." This has not been viewed as a user-friendly idea; for most of us, obtaining the "good life" has been our primary goal.

We are standing at a crossroads. A decision is required. If we decide to go straight ahead, using only our own resources, we can anticipate more of the same. On the other hand, if we decide to change our direction and rely on the power of God's resources, we open up the possibility of a whole new experience. The sole purpose of coming this far was to decide which direction we will take now. The way we came no longer matters. Its purpose was to bring us to where we currently find ourselves.

There is much to celebrate, in that we have achieved a number of material successes. On the other hand, we feel bereft of any *real* joy and happiness from these same successes. The question is simply this: "Do we want more of the same, or do we want to be happy?"

This is the decision we are confronted with. Our joy, happiness, and freedom in life rest upon our answer. It is surely a decision not to be taken lightly or to be put off until some future time. We see the problem. There is a solution. Now is the time to change direction.

Once we decide in favor of happiness, we delegate complete operating authority to God. He is now free to add his expertise and resources to everything we do. All that is required of us is to believe that he can provide the joy, happiness, and freedom we seek, and that we're *willing* to cooperate in the process. Trust him, and watch what happens!

What's Missing in My Life?

Not one single thing! God, by definition, made all things. God makes all things *perfectly* (it is his nature). And, since God made you, *you* must be perfect. Are you? Of course you are! Otherwise there's something wrong with our original proposition. Okay, but why don't you think, or better still, *know* that you're perfect? And, by the way, what does "perfect" mean?

At last, the *real* question: "Who are you?" You are a creation of God, made perfectly in his image (spirit). As such, you possess all of the things (characteristics and capabilities) that he intended for your continued (eternal) enjoyment. He did not make you *incomplete,* in need of finishing the job yourself by finding joy, happiness, and freedom through the acquisition of "things and stuff."

He made each of us with a full complement of joy, happiness, freedom, fulfillment, and inner peace. It's just that we've somehow *misplaced* these things (hence the feeling that *something* is "missing"). And as we feel an absence of these much-desired *feelings,* we seek desperately to experience them through the acquisition of outside things. The problem is that not one of these feelings is the by-product of either career accomplishment or the acquisition of anything.

The big secret is that we already have *everything* we'll ever need—we just don't know it. The only way we can truly come to enjoy these God-given blessings is to *find out who we really are.* And just as soon as we do, *we'll find what we've been looking for!*

There is not one single thing *missing* from your life! God made you perfectly! Believe that you are one of God's children, and that, as such, you are capable of experiencing the feelings of joy, happiness, and freedom, each and every minute of each and every day. Believe it, pray about it, and meditate on it. You'll soon come to *know* it and to live your life to the full, regardless of what "stuff" you have, or have not, acquired. Try it, and see what happens! God blesses you.

Moment of Reflection
"The Power Shift"

Underlying Principle: Commitment, *n.*, the act or process of entrusting or consigning; the state of being committed; an engagement or pledge to do something. *(Standard Encyclopedic Dictionary)*

Implicit Question: Am I prepared to extend an invitation to the God of my understanding to actively participate in my life?

Personal Discovery: Because I've stood at this very same crossroads before and *not* changed direction, why do I think this time will be different?

Related Thought: "In the many adversities and trials of life it is often hard to say 'Thy will be done.' But why not say it? God ever does only what is right and wise and best; what is prompted by a father's love, and what to his children will work out to their highest good."

—Edward Payson (1783–1827)

Fourth Concept:
The Renovation Process

Our invitation to God to join with us in our daily life requires that we review the condition of the "house" we will be sharing. To the extent that we have unfinished projects, shoddy maintenance, and some rather old furnishings, we would certainly want to renovate before he takes up residence. We'd also feel much better about the potential effectiveness of our new relationship if our house was in order. We call this "The Renovation Process."

The problem facing most programs of personal renewal is the high incidence of relapse. Our attempts at New Year's resolutions are a classic example of the high failure rate among participants. The difference between those resolutions and what we're doing in this renovation process is in the high risk associated with our failure. We have been denied our reasonable share of joy, happiness, and freedom for far too long and are not in any way prepared to jeopardize our present and future participation.

As with any renovation program, not all of what is inspected requires repair or replacement. We often find that a significant percentage of what is examined is in very good condition and worthy of retention. These are not the things that give us cause for concern. It is the frayed or faulty wiring that is capable of short-circuiting our best-laid plans that is most in need of repair. We must also look very carefully at the structural support mechanisms that, if in a weakened condition, could result in an untimely collapse.

We need to review our past performances to find out what really makes us "tick." Our inspection will be thorough and searching, for as Socrates said, "The unexamined life is not worth living." Here we examine our life to find out why we are "wired" to act in certain ways. We will look at ourselves objectively, perhaps for the first time, and allow ourselves to make new decisions about future actions. How have we been shaped by major events in our life, and do we find that acceptable?

It's remarkable how good it makes us feel to have spent the time and to have made the effort to "clean house." Unlike spring cleaning, this renovation process is not an annual event. Once completed and our corrections made, it should not be necessary to repeat the process in the foreseeable future. We will have made a pile of all that we no longer wish to hold on to and have taken it to the dumpster. It's an exhilarating feeling!

Cause and Effect

We tend to think that what happens, and the way we feel about it, is the *effect* of what someone else has done to us (*cause*). And we can get very upset about it! Their actions may certainly justify a severe response, either in defense or in retaliation . . . right? Wrong!

What if the way it all works is that we first decide what kind of response we want in our life (*cause*) and then *preset* our "antennae" to pick up only the responses that witness to our need? Aren't *we* then the *cause*, and the response from whomever or whatever, the *effect*? Right!

So just where do we get off holding somebody else responsible for what we wanted (needed) to have happen in our life? If that's how it works, why can't we decide (cause) that we want to have a different effect brought to our attention? We can, simply by making a new decision as to what we want brought to our awareness. Our "antennae" then proceed to search for that kind of response (witness) and bring it to us. The process doesn't change. That's the way it works. The good news is that we control the input (cause). And the process assures the outcome (effect). How great is that?

It all begs the question: "Who should we hold responsible

for what's in our life?" Only ourselves! So let's not be so quick to blame others for our plight. It's only our own "messengers" bringing back what we sent them out to get. Could you but *believe* in the process, just imagine the power you'd have to influence future outcomes. Try it, and see what happens! God blesses you.

Moment of Reflection
"The Renovation Process"

Underlying Principle: Reparations, *n.*, the act of making amends; atonement; repairing or the state of being repaired. (*Standard Encyclopedic Dictionary*)

Implicit Question: Am I willing to critically examine my past behavior pattern in an effort to uncover any errors that may be in need of correction?

Personal Discovery: Do I persist in holding on to my old ideas, expecting to achieve a different result?

Related Thought: "We ought not to look back unless it is to derive useful lessons from past errors, and for the purpose of profiting from our dearly bought experience."

— George Washington (1732–1799)

Fifth Concept: The Release Factor

Having taken an objective look at ourselves, we have probably found a number of things that are in need of correction. We may also have discovered things we have done to others for which we should consider making amends. In fact, truthfully, we would appreciate the opportunity to correct these errors and to offer the appropriate amends to make things right.

Unresolved errors leave us with feelings of guilt. The only way to be released from these feelings is to recognize the *whole truth* of the situation and make whatever reparations are necessary. We tend to have a real problem with the idea of forgiveness—not so much with forgiving others, as we *say* we're always willing to do, but in seeking and accepting forgiveness for ourselves. We'll even get to the point of living with the guilt as the lesser of two "evils." Maybe someday we will get to fix things up and feel better about ourselves. After all, we rationalize, a lot of people have done things to us for which they've never made amends. Unfortunately, this type of rationalization does not relieve our gnawing feelings of guilt. So unless we deal with the *cause* of these feelings, we'll have no choice but to continue to live with them.

We are fortunate indeed that our own forgiveness is not contingent on the "injured" party forgiving us! According to the "Law of Giving," to the extent that we offer forgiveness to others for all of their errors, we will receive it for ourselves. This law is illustrated in the Lord's Prayer, "Forgive us our trespasses as we forgive those who trespass against us." We will come to know, however, that the forgiveness we offer to others must be *total* and from the heart if we are to receive meaningful forgiveness for ourselves. We call this "The Release Factor."

There is an incredible feeling of release experienced through the total forgiveness of others. Within a relatively short period of time, following our forgiveness of others, we will recognize that we too have been forgiven. We sense the lifting of a tremendous weight from our shoulders and begin to experience what freedom really feels like. Incredible indeed!

COACH'S MESSAGE

Circles of Guilt, Blame, and Punishment
. . . by Agreement!

These are the special relationships we have with people we can count on to do their part . . . and not walk away! They support some of the most fundamental ideas that we have about who we are and what's supposed to happen in our lives. They represent the balance of crime and punishment that we require in order to feel comfortable about ourselves, and justified in our own behavior patterns.

The tacit agreement is that because I feel guilty about something that I did (or am doing), you will find an opportunity to blame me for something that you're feeling guilty about and punish me accordingly. This causes me to experience the pain and suffering I deserve. Justice has then been served, and my "debt" is now at least partially paid.

In return for you allowing me to pay my "debt" for the guilt that I was feeling, I agree to blame you for something that I'm feeling guilty about and punish you accordingly. This, then, allows you to experience the pain and suffering necessary to assuage the guilt you're feeling about something you've done. Thus, the reciprocity of our agreement is upheld.

These are often unwritten, unarticulated, and unconscious agreements that, if pointed out, would be met with strenuous defense and denial by either party. Surely two people enjoying a sane relationship would not agree to support one another through providing both the cause and effect required to perpetuate a continued cycle of guilt, blame, and punishment in order to feel better about themselves, would they?

The problem is that once either party withdraws from the arrangement (often as a result of "seeing" the insanity and wanting to find a less destructive way of interacting), the other party is left without a *special relationship* (read: *trusted bad guy*) to "offload" the blame for his or her *own* feelings of guilt. This presents a real disruption to the symbiosis that was relied upon for the continued "support" for behavior problems. And unless *the other person* also makes the decision to change, a real sense of betrayal, frustration, and confusion is destined to follow, compelling him or her to search for a new partner who will allow the "agreement" to be reconstituted.

So the next time you're about to blame someone with whom you have a special relationship—for anything—remember that you may be doing so because you're feeling guilty about your *own* behavior and are looking to provide a source for the punishment you believe you deserve. Don't let yourself be party to an agreement that causes pain and suffering to anyone, let alone yourself or someone you care for! Work on seeing yourself as *not guilty*, and you'll be relieved of the need to place blame elsewhere. Try it, and see what happens! God blesses you.

Moment of Reflection
"The Release Factor"

Underlying Principle: Forgiveness, *n.*, the act of forgiving or the state of being forgiven. (*Oxford Dictionary of Current English,* Third Edition)

Implicit Question: Am I prepared to forgive *all* others for the wrongs that I believe have been done to me?

Personal Discovery: When I tell my "side" of the story, is that *really* what happened, or is it just what I'd like others to *think* happened? How might it sound if I were more honest about my needs?

Related Thought: "It is in vain for you to expect, it is impudent for you to ask of God forgiveness for yourself if you refuse to exercise this forgiving temper as to others."

—Benjamin Hoadley (1676–1761)

Sixth Concept: The Direct Connection

I f we have been thorough in our renovation and forgiveness efforts, we begin to notice a change in ourselves. We have a new feeling of inner peace and can sense the true potential of a life lived with, and directed by, the God of our understanding. Actually, we've been preparing ourselves for something that is truly remarkable: *conscious contact with God!*

The good news is that conscious contact with God is achievable. In fact, it is one of the most natural abilities available to us, given our direct descendents. The bad news is we either don't know it or haven't developed the skills required to communicate with him directly. Conscious contact with God allows us to discover our true potential and to create successful outcomes and good fortune with effortless ease. We call this "The Direct Connection."

The problem is that we're using *conditioned responses* to deal with the events of the day rather than bringing them to God and asking for direction. God wants us to have everything our hearts desire. In fact, all of his phenomenal resources are consistently applied to just that purpose. The only thing that prevents the realization of our desires is our *other* agenda, which is often kept secret from our own conscious awareness, and definitely kept from God's.

When we bring everything to God and seek his direction, we shine a light on the entire subject matter and position ourselves to experience the best possible outcome. It is now time to let go of our old ideas and allow God to enter our hearts and lives, as we have never before imagined.

Just how do we contact God directly? Actually, it's quite simple; the tools we use are prayer and meditation. Prayer is *talking* to God, and meditation is *listening* to him. We need to set aside a specific time each morning for this important communication. It's a very small investment of time that will pay huge dividends as our day progresses.

Establishing conscious contact with God has a profound effect on our everyday confidence and enthusiasm for life. It's not long before we begin to see that things seem to work out better than they used to. People appear to be more understanding, and our enjoyment of life is greatly enhanced. God seems to go before us and prepare the way. And he opens doors we didn't even know were there. For results like these, our morning communication is *imperative!*

Changing the Operating System
in Our Personal Computer

It seems that we perform much like the computers we've become so dependent upon. As our computer ages and we finally recognize that its output capabilities are no longer meeting our objectives, it's time to upgrade the operating system.

We experience such an exhilarating feeling as we watch the old system being deleted from our central processing unit, and the new one being installed. With every change, we have the expectation that our future performance will be so much better than it had been in the past. This is true especially if we've been diligent in our search, seeking only to find a system that includes the entire range of features deemed to be desirable.

We also know that our first attempts to actually operate the new system will be somewhat hesitant, as we're unsure of what we're doing and have not as yet gained the confidence that comes from familiarity with the process. However, as we witness the early results produced from our efforts, we're excited about both the hope and the promise of what's to come. There is no question that this is a *new beginning!*

This computer upgrade scenario is a perfect metaphor for

"deleting" our *conditioned mind* (read: *old* operating system) from controlling the response we have to situations and events in our everyday life and replacing it with a *spiritual awakening* (read: *new* operating system). The results will be even more spectacular, and the "upgrade" will last throughout eternity! There is no question that this too is a *new beginning!* Try it, and see what happens! God blesses you.

Moment of Reflection
"The Direct Connection"

Underlying Principle: Knowledge, *n.*, information or awareness acquired through experience or education; deep and extensive learning; the sum of what is known.

Implicit Question: Am I confident that I know where to go, what to do, what to say, and who to say it to?

Personal Discovery: If I'm not relying on the Source of *all* knowledge for guidance and direction, to what or to whom am I entrusting my life?

Related Thought: "The wise man is but a clever infant, spelling letters from a hieroglyphical prophetic book, the lexicon of which lies in eternity."

—Thomas Carlyle (1795–1881)

Seventh Concept: The 200 Percent Life

We began with the realization that no amount of career or material success could ever bring us the joy, happiness, and freedom we sought. We've come a long way. We defined our God, invited him to join in our lives, and empowered him to act on our behalf. We took a personal inventory of ourselves, made reparations where necessary, and received forgiveness through extending it to others. We established a morning routine that included both prayer and meditation, enabling us to make conscious contact with God for daily guidance and direction.

Each one of these concepts was essential to discovering the 100 percent of our spiritual reality that provides us with the joy of life. And when this is combined with the 100 percent of our material life, we begin to experience what we call, "The 200 Percent Life."

There is no lack of joy, happiness, and freedom, or any scarcity of resources, in a life lived with God and guided by spiritual principles. It allows us to have and enjoy both happiness and material success at the same time, each on its own level. This was our real goal from the beginning, and its achievement is now clearly in sight. As we live the 200 Percent Life, our attitude and outlook on life will change. We will experience joy, happiness, and freedom in our daily lives, and know inner peace. That awful gut feeling that *something is missing* will leave us. We will intuitively know how to handle situations that used to baffle us. The enjoyment of our material success will be greatly enhanced, not only for us, but also for our loved ones. We will enjoy the benefit of an unlimited supply of *all* that we desire and recognize that God is doing everything for us that we were unable to do for ourselves.

COACH'S MESSAGE

What's So Exciting About Searching for a Buried Treasure?

Finding such a treasure would surely bring us the joy, happiness, and freedom we seek! And that's absolutely true . . . as long as the treasure we find is the very thing that does indeed allow us to experience such feelings. *Most don't!*

The visions we have in contemplating a treasure find are generally associated with finding a chest chock-full of "golden doubloons" buried by a famous pirate marauder, or a vault full of "golden statuary" buried with an ancient king. Wealth beyond our wildest dreams! And, of course, the joy, happiness, and freedom that would accompany the newfound wealth!

And it's these same things we're looking for in the much less exotic searching we engage in every day of our lives. Whether it's a promotion, a new car, a new lover, a vacation, or simply recognition for something that we've accomplished, all have the same common objective: to *acquire something* and the hope that that acquisition will bring us the happiness we seek.

Unfortunately, it's not going to happen. Happiness is not a by-product of the acquisition of *anything!* Each of us was endowed with a full complement of joy, happiness, and freedom in the beginning that we have forgotten or somehow overlooked. These things are exactly what God *intended us to enjoy,* each and every moment of each and every day, forever!

Instead of seeking happiness by discovering gold coins or artifacts in a buried treasure, or through any other form of material acquisition, we need only look *inside* and discover the "buried treasure" of who we really are. *For just as soon as we find out who we really are, we'll find what we've been looking for!* This is, by far, the greatest and most fruitful treasure hunt you could ever undertake. Try it, and see what happens! God blesses you.

Moment of Reflection
"The 200 Percent Life"

Underlying Principle: Fulfillment, n., satisfaction resulting from fully developing one's abilities; the accomplishment of something promised.

Implicit Question: Am I enjoying the presence of everything that my *heart* desires?

Personal Discovery: If the "hose that waters the garden" is not flowing to its full potential, could it be that I have my "foot" on it?

Related Thought: "Plenty and indigence depend upon the opinion everyone has of them; and riches, like glory or health, have no more beauty or pleasure, than their possessor is pleased to lend them."

—Michel E. de Montaigne (1533–1592)

Part IV
THE SEVEN STRATEGIES

First Strategy: Know Yourself

One of the greatest questions of all time is, "Who are you?" Many of us respond with our name, job title, and place of work. This is what we *do*, not who we *are!* Others of us will quote our name, residence, and family status, which are what we *have*, not who we *are!* Why is it so difficult to answer the question precisely? Because we tend to describe ourselves in relation to other people's interest in us, or our interest in them, rather than describing who we *really* are.

The problem is that few of us have any idea who we really are. It's often not until midlife that we even give it much thought. We're all familiar with the successful person who tells us, "I'm taking a year off and going to Europe to find myself." This begs the question, "Who's lost?" The short answer is that no one is *lost* in God's awareness, but God has been lost in *our* awareness.

One of the misconceptions of life is that we are human beings having a spiritual experience, when, in reality, we're spiritual beings having a human experience. Is it any wonder, then, that we become confused, frustrated, and even angry when our best human efforts and applied wisdom do not bring the satisfaction we seek? The gut feeling that *something is missing* in our life is our "self" seeking its own identity.

When we find out who we really are, we'll find what we've been looking for! Our task is a simple one; not easy, but simple. We need to recognize our *true* identity and live life through our spiritual reality. We receive an incredible blessing when we discover the complete fulfillment that is, and always has been, our birthright. It is only when we apply spiritual principles to our human objectives that the outcomes include joy, happiness, and freedom. There is one promise that we can totally rely on: "Seek and you shall find." It therefore augurs well that we are now seeking.

COACH'S MESSAGE

Seek . . . and You Shall Find!

This is a spiritual statement of promise, yet one that is often met with confusion. The response that I hear most frequently to this statement is, "I know, but *where* do I seek?" To this I reply, "I don't know, but you do!" This is often followed by, "No, I don't!" and me saying, "Oh yes, you do!"

The reason *you,* and *only you* can possibly know *where* to seek, is because *you're* the one who decides *what* it is you're *truly* looking for. And once you've identified that—and just exactly what may be keeping you from it—you will be moved to begin your search in earnest.

Quite possibly, and probably, this will be in a whole new direction from where you may have been looking previously. It *doesn't matter* where that is—it *only matters* that you begin the search! You'll be shown where to go next, and what you need to do will be made perfectly clear to you by your *"internal guide"* (the Holy Spirit).

How could anyone, other than yourself, possibly tell you what you're looking for, let alone *where* to look for it? It would exhibit the height of arrogance for anyone to presume *they* know—to say nothing about how you would be abdicating your personal responsibility for discovering who you really are, and as Deepak Chopra says, "becoming the author of your own existence."

So if you sense that something is keeping you from the enjoyment of life, and you're not too sure what it might be, or where to look for it, ask the *only* person who could possibly know: *yourself!* Try it, and see what happens! God blesses you.

Applying the Strategy
"Know Yourself"

Practical Consideration:

• When I say I'm a "human being," what is it that's the "human" part? What's the "being" part?

• If God were to brag about me to someone, calling me his favorite child, what would he say is the phase I'm going through? And what would he say I'm going to *be* when I grow up?

• If God is "King" and I am his son, then it follows that I'm a prince, and as such, I live in a beautiful palace and am heir to the entire "kingdom." Why do I *choose* to live in the basement of the palace, clutching the few trinkets I have at hand?

Personal Application:

• When I ask myself what it is about money that's important to me, what's the answer? Then, when I ask myself what is important to me about that response, what is my answer? Continuing with this line of inquiry until I can't go any further, what's the *one* thing that's *really important* to me?

- As God made me who I am, I will stop comparing myself to other people. It's a loser's game. If, by comparison, I fall short, I'll feel inferior. If I come out ahead, I'll feel superior. Either way I lose!

- Because I'm not *really* the secular/hedonistic person I've been masquerading as, I'll give up my personal "story," complete with all its problems and self-protecting rationalizations, and begin anew.

Pertinent Quotation:

"We shall not cease from exploration / And the end of all our exploring / Will be to arrive where we started / And know the place for the first time."

—T. S. Eliot (1888–1965)

Second Strategy: Choose Your God

Our approach to God is by way of personal spiritual experience rather than religious doctrine or theory. We believe that while a universal *theology* is impossible, a universal *spiritual awareness* is not only possible, it is necessary to the achievement of a common spiritual objective, regardless of the chosen path.

Experience has shown that the best way to choose a path to God is to first revisit the relationship (if any) we currently have with him. We need to ask ourselves: Does my current relationship allow me to experience the joy, happiness, and freedom that I was endowed with in the very beginning? If the answer is "yes," we are blessed indeed, and should continue on the chosen path. However, if the answer is "no," we need to challenge ourselves to develop a new relationship that does. This will require that we drill down into our belief system and examine each one of our old ideas about who we *thought* God was, and exchange them for who he really is.

It's critical to achieving our stated goals that the character-istics we ascribe to the God of our understanding be fully aligned with our willingness to cooperate with him, as he can only accomplish that which we will *allow* him to do, and noth-ing more. We need to clarify precisely what it is that we believe God can do for us, and proclaim our faith in his ability to succeed.

This is the moment most of us have been waiting for. This is no time to be timid in our requests. On the contrary, it is the precise time to express our genuine desire and intention to experience the joy, happiness, and freedom of our endowment. We're now about to travel on the road to realization!

Why Does Anyone Want to Have God in His or Her Life?

They probably don't! What they've come to understand is that they've been unable to experience any real happiness or a true sense of personal fulfillment through their current belief system. And having pretty much exhausted all alternative strategies, they've become *willing* to at least (and at last) consider "The God Thing."

A good number of us seem to come to God "kicking and screaming," all but convinced that the "good life" we've been pursuing will probably be over if we turn to him! However, in the interest of finding *happiness*, we'll give up the "good life." Does this make any sense at all? Only to the insane! Perhaps we need to revisit our definition of what enjoying a "good life" really means.

I used to define the "good life" as having the appearance of success. Perhaps this would include a promotion with the appropriate increase in income, or having a home, driving a car, and owning a wide selection of "toys," which would be the envy of my contemporaries. Looking good in the mirror and dressing to impress would be important too. I would definitely be a person who you would want to include among your more accomplished acquaintances! The only thing that seemed to be missing from this equation was that I never felt any *real happiness* in my life, irrespective of my career accomplishments and material acquisitions.

In retrospect, I can see why these "successes" were unable to provide the happiness I sought . . . and why they never would. The reason, quite simply, is that happiness is not the by-product of the acquisition of anything! We were *endowed* with perfect joy, happiness, and freedom *in the beginning*, directly from God, which we have either misplaced or forgotten. Our task is to *rediscover* who we really are, and when we do, *we'll find what we've been looking for!*

Today, with God in my life, enjoying the "good life" means that I've been blessed with a knowing-feeling of joy, happiness, and freedom, each and every moment of each and every day, regardless of the situation in which I find myself. I meet life with a childlike enthusiasm, in constant amazement of the incredible workings of my God.

While enjoying the use of a full measure of the material things produced by a modern society, I am at the same time blessed with the inner peace and sense of personal fulfillment that surpasses all understanding. My "ladder" is now leaning against the *right* "building," and I know that when I finally reach the top of the "ladder," I'll be *exactly* where I want to be!

So . . . why might you want to have God in your life? If you're anything like I was, you probably don't! What you want is to be joyous, happy, and free in all that you do. The trouble is that it's only through awareness of your true relationship with God that the knowing-feeling of these blessings is experienced. What's your definition of the "good life"? Perhaps you may wish to revisit the term. Try it, and see what happens! God blesses you.

Applying the Strategy
"Choose Your God"

Practical Consideration:

• Am I prepared to develop a more meaningful relationship with the God of my understanding?

• Does my current understanding of God represent the God I would *personally* choose? If so, how so? If not, why not?

• Are the attributes that I ascribe to the God of my understanding aligned with my willingness to fully cooperate with him?

Personal Application:

• Before recruiting to fill the "God" position in my life, I will prepare a job description and define the requisite qualifications.

• It is essential that I clearly articulate exactly what it is I want God to do for me, in both the short and long term. Making a list is the most effective way to reveal my *intentions*, and to focus my *attention*.

Applying the Strategy
"Choose Your God" *(cont'd)*

• Once I have chosen my God, and outlined his mandate, I will meet with him privately to formally engage his services, and to establish a protocol for performance reporting.

Pertinent Quotation:

"Who guides below and rules above, the great disposer and the mighty king; than he none greater; next him none can be, or is, or was; supreme, he singly fills the throne."

—Horace (65 BCE–8 CE)

Third Strategy: Delegate Authority

If our chosen God is all we have described him as being, then it follows that we should entrust him with the responsibility for performance. Applying his resources to any given situation allows a far greater potential for success and the best possible outcome. To do anything other than that, from the standpoint of logic alone, would be to assure a lesser result.

As any good manager knows, adequate authority must accompany responsibility for performance. This requires us to delegate full operating authority to God, as we understand him, so he may carry out his mandate.

The problem most of us have in delegating authority is our fear of loss of control. Our conditioned minds tend to suggest that he might not be fully aware of the history of this particular situation, and it might be better if we took over. However, we must resolve this dilemma in favor of God if we are to achieve the results we hope for. As we have been in the practice of "controlling" the outcome of our activities in the past, this may not be an easy adjustment to make, but make it we must! We need to be vigilant in keeping our commitment to allow our God to control the game.

If our God is both all-knowing and all-powerful, the outcome of any action must be exactly as it is supposed to be. If it is not as we had anticipated, rest assured that there is a greater good being served. It could even be something outside of our current awareness, the specifics of which may never be known to us.

God has three possible answers to everything we ask of him: "yes," "no," and "not yet." The answer that we tend to have the most trouble with is the last one. We can generally handle a "yes" or a "no," but it's the "not yet" answer that baffles us. Instead of accepting that the time is not *right* for whatever it is to happen, we regroup and begin a new offensive to *make* it happen. Should we be "successful" in forcing it to happen, it could prove to be detrimental to our overall well-being.

Remember, "God guides, God provides." Learning to trust God is one of the highest goals to which we can aspire, as well as one of the most rewarding. Relax, and enjoy the trip.

God Guides, God Provides!

What does this maxim mean to you? Actually, it has every-thing to do with whether or not you've made the *decision* to turn your life over to God! This decision greatly influences the kind of experience you can expect from your next project or interaction with someone.

If it's something you're doing on your own, as a *self-reliant* individual, you'll have to plan all of the inputs, gauge the response you expect to receive, interpret the motives of others who might respond to you, and judge whether or not they did the "right" thing. You will then match the results to your expec-tations and determine whether or not you're satisfied with the outcome. All in all, this can be a very demanding exercise, accompanied by a high degree of anxiety.

Or, you can first run it by God to get a sense if it's the right thing to say or do in a particular situation. Then, if you believe that it is, you can ask God to go before you and prepare the way, and to help you do the best you can with what you have (not with what you used to have, or some-day you might have, but with what you have today), with whatever he puts in front of you! Now you can relax and enjoy the trip, because *you* do not have to "make it all happen." That's God's job . . . let him do it!

What you'll notice is that everything seems to work out very well, even better than you might have hoped for. And it's all done with the sense of inner peace and feelings of joy, happiness, and freedom. Is there something else that you want? Try it, and see what happens! God blesses you.

Applying the Strategy
"Delegate Authority"

Practical Consideration:

• What fears surface when I think about turning my *complete* life over to God? What do I *believe* I'm better able to handle?

• Is it rational for me to believe that with God controlling the "game," I will no longer be able to participate in what is often described as the "good life"? Might I benefit from revisiting my definition of the term?

• What does the maxim "God guides, God provides" suggest to me in terms of delegating authority?

Personal Application:

• I will reevaluate both the *positive* and *negative* results I've experienced through the use of what, up until now, has been the "driving force" in my life.

Applying the Strategy
"Delegate Authority" (cont'd)

- It will be most helpful for me to make a list of all of the things I'll be turning over to God. The more specific and thorough the list, the more effective it will be.

- After one year, when I'm looking back on having delegated complete operating authority to God, what are some of the things that would have had to happen for me to regard it as a success?

Pertinent Quotation:

"See God on both sides of the table. Claim that God is working through both of you. . . . Then if you don't make that sale, you'll make a better one instead. If you don't get the job, you'll get a better one. If you don't make the arrangement that you sought today, a better one will present itself tomorrow."

—Emmet Fox (1886–1951)

Fourth Strategy: Personal Inventory

Every successful business periodically takes an inventory of its merchandise. It must determine not only what is in stock, but also the condition of the goods. That which is salable will be retained, while damaged goods will be either repaired or discarded. The future profitability of the business depends on both the thoroughness and honesty with which the inventory is taken.

This same principle holds true for taking our personal inventory. Our *salable* assets are our positive behaviors, business acumen, interpersonal skills, intellectual understanding, good health, compassionate demeanor, and our grateful attitude. Our *damaged* goods include detrimental behavior patterns, areas of poor performance, attitudinal difficulties, unresolved emotional stresses, anger, and resentments. These lists are by no means exhaustive, but rather indicative of the kinds of inventory items that need to be thoroughly reviewed if we are to operate *profitably* in the future.

One of the problems we encounter in taking a personal inventory is our tendency to blame some of our difficulties on other people. This often happens when we discover areas of dishonesty or self-seeking in our own behavior. However, as our best results will come from an honest assessment of *our* behavior, we are well advised to remember that this exercise is a *personal* inventory, and the role that others may have played is not our current concern. At best it distracts us from our desired outcome; at worst it can be misleading or harmful.

It is a spiritual axiom that you can't solve a problem with the same mind that created it. It therefore follows that if we're to solve our behavioral problems, we will have to *change* our minds. Once we have the results of our personal inventory, we will be required to give careful consideration to each and every item in the damaged section, so they can either be corrected or discarded. Either action requires that we change our mind about how we will proceed in the future. The results we achieve will be the "barometer" of our thoroughness and honesty.

Taking a personal inventory puts us in the enviable position of being able to make *new* choices. It is precisely these new choices that will allow us to both improve and enjoy our future performance. An examined life is indeed worth living!

COACH'S MESSAGE

How Do You Get Rid of Darkness?

By meeting it with light! Just as soon as you turn on the light, the darkness *vanishes*. Yet, when it comes to dealing with problems ("darkness") affecting our personal lives, we tend to search for some complex or disciplined "fix" for resolution. In reality, all that's necessary to remove the darkness is to *bring light to the problem*. When light is shone on darkness, darkness disappears.

How simple is that? As a matter of fact, it's so simple that God uses it to solve and resolve every problem or situation in which we may find ourselves. No matter how difficult the task or how horrendous the potential consequences, all that God asks of us is that we *bring the problem to light*. It is at that very instant that we recognize and acknowledge that there is indeed a problem—and the extent of it—that the resolution process begins!

It is only when we refuse to recognize and acknowledge a problem, *thus keeping it in darkness*, that it is unresolved. It will be repeated again and again until it is finally *brought to light*. This will definitely happen; it's just a matter of time. We get to decide how long we need to have the "benefits" the problem provides for us, although this will not be in our conscious awareness.

81

Even if we claim otherwise, there are indeed benefits accompanying any problem. Somehow, in some very real way, there is a *payoff* that we receive from the presence of our "selected" problems with which we seem to be afflicted. Bringing them to the light includes an honest assessment of what it is we seem to be "getting" from the problem that requires us to continue the process. This discovery and acknowledgment is the very "light" that will remove the darkness. Try it, and see what happens! God blesses you.

READER/CUSTOMER CARE SURVEY

We care about your opinions! Please take a moment to fill out our online Reader Survey at **http://survey.hcibooks.com**.
As a **"THANK YOU"** you will receive a **VALUABLE INSTANT COUPON** towards future book purchases
as well as a **SPECIAL GIFT** available only online! Or, you may mail this card back to us.

(PLEASE PRINT IN ALL CAPS)

First Name _____ MI. _____ Last Name _____

Address _____

State _____ Zip _____ Email _____ City _____

1. Gender
☐ Female   ☐ Male

2. Age
☐ 8 or younger
☐ 9-12   ☐ 13-16
☐ 17-20   ☐ 21-30
☐ 31+

3. Did you receive this book as a gift?
☐ Yes   ☐ No

4. Annual Household Income
☐ under $25,000
☐ $25,000 - $34,999
☐ $35,000 - $49,999
☐ $50,000 - $74,999
☐ over $75,000

5. What are the ages of the children living in your house?
☐ 0 - 14   ☐ 15+

6. Marital Status
☐ Single
☐ Married
☐ Divorced
☐ Widowed

7. How did you find out about the book?
(please choose one)
☐ Recommendation
☐ Store Display
☐ Online
☐ Catalog/Mailing
☐ Interview/Review

8. Where do you usually buy books?
(please choose one)
☐ Bookstore
☐ Online
☐ Book Club/Mail Order
☐ Price Club (Sam's Club, Costco's, etc.)
☐ Retail Store (Target, Wal-Mart, etc.)

9. What subject do you enjoy reading about the most?
(please choose one)
☐ Parenting/Family
☐ Relationships
☐ Recovery/Addictions
☐ Health/Nutrition
☐ Christianity
☐ Spirituality/Inspiration
☐ Business Self-help
☐ Women's Issues
☐ Sports

10. What attracts you most to a book?
(please choose one)
☐ Title
☐ Cover Design
☐ Author
☐ Content

TAPE IN MIDDLE; DO NOT STAPLE

BUSINESS REPLY MAIL
FIRST-CLASS MAIL   PERMIT NO 45   DEERFIELD BEACH, FL

POSTAGE WILL BE PAID BY ADDRESSEE

Health Communications, Inc.
3201 SW 15th Street
Deerfield Beach FL 33442-9875

IｨᵘＩｨᵘᵘＩＩＩｨᵘＩｨᵘᵘＩｨᵘｨＩＩＩＩｨᵘᵘＩｨᵘＩＩＩｨᵘＩｨＩＩＩＩ

FOLD HERE

Comments

Applying the Strategy
"Personal Inventory"

Practical Consideration:

• How many times have I caught myself exclaiming, "I can't believe I did that *again!*" Could it be the result of not having made any changes in my behavior?

• If my God-given talents have allowed me to enjoy success in my *material* life, why have I been so hesitant in adapting these same talents to the benefit of my *spiritual* life?

• How have I been shaped by major events in my life, and do I find that acceptable?

Personal Application:

• Undertaking a thorough and objective review of my past performances will help to identify unfavorable behavior patterns and point toward the changes necessary to improve future performance.

Applying the Strategy
"Personal Inventory" (cont'd)

- I will resist the tendency to blame some of my difficulties on other people, particularly as I discover areas of dishonesty or self-seeking in my own behavior, as it can be misleading or harmful to my desired outcome.

- As motivation is always a drive toward being better, unconsciously driven motivation leads to the constant feeling that something is missing. By uncovering my *hidden motivators*, there exists the possibility of experiencing a sense of continuous achievement.

Pertinent Quotation:

"It is our own past which has made us what we are. We are the children of our own deeds. Conduct has created character; acts have grown into habits; each year has pressed into us a deeper moral print; the lives we have led have left us such as we are today."

—John B. Dykes (1823–1876)

Fifth Strategy: Forgiveness

The Golden Rule is perhaps one of the most well-known spiritual principles of all time: Do unto others as you would have them do unto you. It is generally agreed that this is the appropriate way to treat other people. What is not so well known is that it is a spiritual law (the Law of Giving) mandating that "as you give, so shall you receive."

Therefore, if you want forgiveness, forgive others; if you want freedom, give freedom to others; if you want attention and appreciation, learn to give attention and appreciation; and if you want material affluence, help others to become materially affluent. In fact, the easiest way to get what you want is to give it away! This "dynamic exchange" is the direct effect of the Law of Giving.

Unfortunately, although most of us understand this phenomenon *intellectually*, we have not adapted it *beneficially* in our everyday lives. Actually, we all too frequently use this spiritual law against ourselves by misunderstanding its full implications. When we attempt to justify the projection of guilt onto others so that we may feel free of it, a "boomerang" effect is automatically established. We then sense our own sinfulness, carry its guilt, and expect to be punished accordingly—and we will be. It's the law! We get back in direct proportion what we give out. Therefore, we must be very selective in what we give to others.

We are responsible for whatever is in our lives! What wonderful news for those of us who have always sought to be in full control. We were terribly upset when we thought others were responsible for what had happened to us. However, since we are the authors of our own scripts, what we thought was being done to us we actually did to ourselves, though not with conscious intent.

Given this reality, we need to forgive other people for what they *did not do* to us, not what they *did* to us! Our prayer could properly be: "God, help me to forgive all of the people for the errors that *I* have made." This correctly represents what must happen if we are responsible for writing our own script. We need to stop blaming others for outcomes that were required in our life!

Once we understand who writes the script, we have the opportunity to positively affect everything that we do and everyone we come in contact with. This is perhaps the greatest single lesson we can learn in life, and it certainly makes the discipline and effort required to learn it well worth a candle.

Suffering Has Nothing to Do with Pain!

Unless you *want* to "suffer." Or, even worse, unless you want to be *seen to be suffering!* Everyone knows what pain feels like. We've all experienced it, and it hurts. However, some of us feel the pain and *we don't suffer!* Others feel the pain and want to show you just how much they are suffering. Why the difference?

The first group has nothing to gain from showing you that they're suffering from the pain they feel. It just hurts. They know it and are willing to share that information with you. But they're not suffering. Do they want your sympathy? Not really; just your best wishes that the pain will soon stop, and maybe to have you "kiss it better."

The second group has much to gain from demonstrating that their pain is indeed making them suffer. They're not only soliciting your sympathy for their plight, they want you to fully appreciate the difficulty that has been placed upon them. And, most often, that the difficulty is not their fault.

The payoff for them is that the more pain and suffering they can demonstrate, the more "heroic" they appear to be. The overt message to others is: "Look at what I'm having to deal with!" But the *underlying* statement is: "As you witness my suffering, you will not only be sympathetic to my situation, you will consider me to be a 'good' person, *helpless* in fixing the problem and therefore *blameless* for anything else for which I may be responsible." The continuing dialogue will have you saying how sorry you are for their suffering and them telling you it's "okay" and that they're trying their best to cope with it! ("But be sure that you see just exactly *how much* I'm suffering!")

I'm not sure that we're being kind if we fall into that "sympathy trap." In the terminology of transactional analysis, this is called giving someone "sick strokes." You're rewarding them (psychologically) by acknowledging their pseudo-heroism, whereas the very reason for their "plight" is a *charade* for them to feel better about their feelings of low self-esteem and inadequacy. This is not the healthiest way for someone to be dealing with his or her feelings.

So if you're experiencing pain, it's *enough* that it hurts—don't extend the pain into suffering. Deal with it in a more constructive way. And if it's happening to others, treat them with the understanding that they're also God's children, and whatever reason they may have for demonstrating their suffering, it's not something that God willed to be in their life. Therefore, ask God to "forgive them, as they do not know what they do" (Luke 23:34). And, while you're at it, tell him that you also forgive them. Try it, and see what happens! God blesses you.

Applying the Strategy
"Forgiveness"

Practical Consideration:

• Why do I find it so hard to forgive? Is it because there's a certain justification for my actions in feeling that I've been wronged?

• Given that I'm responsible for *everything* that comes into my life, how can I possibly hold other people accountable to *me* for their actions?

• If I'm to do unto others as I would have them do unto me, how might my approach to them change if I saw each one of them as wearing a nametag with my name on it?

Personal Application:

• I will make a list of all the people with whom I have unresolved issues. This information will assist me in determining the extent to which forgiveness may be required.

Applying the Strategy
"Forgiveness" (cont'd)

- In seeking forgiveness for something I did that may have *harmed* someone, I will first determine *precisely* what it was that happened, and what could be done, *specifically*, to correct it. After doing this, I'll make the necessary amends, *directly*, at my earliest opportunity.

- At the end of each day, I will review the events of the day to determine if there is anything for which I need to either forgive or seek forgiveness. If so, whatever correction is deemed to be necessary is to be done without delay.

Pertinent Quotation:

"Retribution is one of the grand principles in the divine administration of human affairs; a requital is imperceptible only to the willfully unobservant. There is everywhere the working of the everlasting law of requital: man always gets as he gives."

—John Foster (1836–1917)

Sixth Strategy: Prayer and Meditation

Words are still the principal means of our communication, while silence is the language of the Spirit. Therefore, as we have invited God into our lives, we are confronted with a communications challenge. We need to use words to speak to God, through prayer, while he uses silence to speak to us, through meditation. It is therefore crucial to our spiritual progress that we become fluently bilingual.

The problem for most of us is being unpracticed in the effective use of prayer and meditation. Our prayers have generally taken the form of supplications, seeking favor for our current situation. This is a contradiction of who we really are and of our absolute birthright, which grants us the full support of all of God's resources. We need only to ask for his guidance and for the strength, power, and ability to carry it out.

Many of us have had little or no instruction in meditative techniques. Our early attempts at meditation were often ineffectual, as we were unable to still our active minds. We also weren't exactly sure what we were supposed to be experiencing. This undisciplined approach made the whole process difficult, if not impossible. Now that we understand prayer and meditation more fully, we meet with God each morning to seek his guidance. This meeting takes place immediately after rising, before the pressures of the day descend upon us. We review the upcoming events and ask for direction in all we plan to do. Clarity of the action required comes through the use of both prayer and meditation. This process moves our words *out* and his guidance *in*. Only then are we properly prepared to meet the events of the day with the expectation of a successful result.

As we learn to use prayer and meditation effectively, we see how easily and effortlessly positive results are achieved. God's participation assures us that whatever we do will be fully supported from inception to completion. When we contrast this idea with the fact that whatever we do alone requires our continued attention and effort, we begin to understand the practical implications of the process. Increased confidence and far less anxiety are but two of the many benefits.

The Language of the Spirit Is Silence

So why do we use both prayer and meditation to communicate with God? Because most of us don't want to "hear" from God until we've finished *telling* him what it is we're interested in having happen! Then we strain, in silent desperation, to hear how he plans to go about doing what we want and what our role is to be in the process. Is it any wonder, then, that we're disappointed when our prayers seem to go unanswered?

Burt Harding, of the Awareness Foundation, pointed out in a recent satsang writing that *silence* is the one thing that destroys the egoic mind. If that is true, and I believe it is, the more our prayers are influenced by our *conditioned mind* (ego), expressing what it is *we want to happen,* the more silence (meditation) will be necessary to offset (destroy) our egoic wishes. Only then does God have any chance of getting through to us, telling us what may indeed be the best course of action.

The lesson I take from this experience is to heed the spiritual wisdom of praying only for knowledge of God's will for me, and to have the strength, power, and ability to carry it out, regardless of the situation in which I may find myself.

Admitting that I really don't know what should or should not be done is much more effective than telling him what to do (ego), and expecting him to find a way to do it.

I now try to leave the ego out of the entire process, allowing God a *barrier-free* opportunity to "speak" to me directly in the silence of meditation. I do this mediation without having to overcome my *predetermined* solution, which was a product of my *personal wisdom!*

So if you're not "hearing" the answers you're looking for when you sit down with God in prayer, perhaps you may be making the mistake of bringing the *answer* to the meeting, rather than the *question!* Try shortening the *talking* time with God and expanding your *listening* time. It may improve your "hearing." Try it, and see what happens! God blesses you.

Applying the Strategy
"Prayer and Meditation"

Practical Consideration:

• Are my prayers to God only to know his will for me and to have the strength, power, and ability to carry it out? Or do I have another agenda?

• If I agree that the *language* of the Spirit is silence, have I been giving God enough quiet time to ensure a reasonable measure of guidance?

• Have I noticed the most *meaningful* moments in my life were not planned by me, but came easily into my awareness in response to a heartfelt desire? Who do I think did the planning and made all of the arrangements?

Personal Application:

• I will set aside a specific time each morning to meet with my God and to seek direction for the day through both prayer and meditation.

Applying the Strategy
"Prayer and Meditation" *(cont'd)*

• When I speak to God in prayer, I will acknowledge each anticipated event in the day, ask him to help me to know his will, and to have the strength, power, and ability to carry it out.

• Before starting my meditation, I will ask God to help me to remember who I *really* am and to speak to my heart. Although his response may not be immediately discernible to me, I will trust that the direction I need will subsequently become clear.

Pertinent Quotation:

"There is no thought in any mind, but it quickly tends to convert itself into a power, and organizes a huge instrumentality of means."

—Ralph Waldo Emerson (1803–1882)

Seventh Strategy: Total Detachment

The main reason we seek to increase our material success is to achieve a sense of personal security. But can the world give us security? Security is a spiritual knowing-feeling that can only exist when we no longer care about worldly security. Is it any wonder spiritual enlightenment is so rare?

As long as we believe that our security is *contingent* upon acquiring or retaining anything, we will be subject to feelings of insecurity, no matter how great our wealth. This in no way is to suggest that we will feel insecure by acquiring or retaining anything. It simply says that if we *believe* our security is contingent on these things, we will feel insecure. There is a huge difference between these two positions. It's the difference between inner peace and constant anxiety.

Seeking security through the acquisition of things is like chasing the horizon. We see it just ahead: then, as we approach, it moves a little farther away. As we try again to approach it, it moves yet again. It's impossible to reach the horizon, no matter how far we travel. The horizon, like the feeling of security, is not a *thing* that can be acquired: it can only be experienced.

Buddha said, "Detachment is the essence of spiritual enlightenment." It is a message that can lead us to the awareness of the God-given inner peace we were meant to know from the beginning. By practicing nonattachment, or, as Buddha called it, detachment to *anything* that comes into our life, we are not only free to fully enjoy its presence, but also to never experience a sense of loss in its absence. This is a spiritual blessing that can *only* be appreciated through total detachment.

Security is a feeling that emanates from a deep and profound knowing-feeling that nothing we gain or lose has the power to affect our personal well-being. The reality is God gave us everything we would ever need to assure our security and enjoyment of life. We do not have to acquire or achieve *anything* to experience the joy, happiness, and freedom that are ours. What we need is to sharpen our awareness, be open to all things, *and be attached to nothing!*

COACH'S MESSAGE

You're Richer than You Think!

At least that's what one of our major banks is advertising. It seems they're able to recognize, through a close analysis of our financial affairs, unused or misused "resources" and deploy them to our greater financial benefit. Hence, their slogan: *"You're richer than you think!"*

It's also a slogan that would be entirely appropriate for adoption by any spiritual advisor. For just as soon as we *uncover* (read: recognize and believe) the blessings that God endowed us with in the beginning, we make a quantum leap in the enjoyment of our everyday life. We truly are much *richer* than we think!

Over the millennia, we have somehow lost sight of who we really are and how God *intended* we should live our lives. As a loving Father, capable of extending *precisely* what he would have us enjoy, he blessed us eternally with *everything* we would ever need. And, through seeking *first* the kingdom of God, as instructed in the New Testament of the Bible, we are promised that "all of these things *shall* be added to us" [my emphasis].

That being the case, why is it we have to fight so hard to achieve even a little peace of mind and a modicum of security? Great question—only it's not the right one! Think about it. If God blessed us with everything we would ever need, *we already have it* and there is nothing to acquire! The real question is, "Why do we *think* there is?"

The answer is both simple and complex: simple, because having forgotten who we really are, we've *abandoned* our inheritance as children of God, and complex because instead of looking "inside" to discover who we really are and enjoying a life of inner peace and security that surpasses all understanding, we busy ourselves in a desperate "outside" search for the unattainable goal of worldly security.

So the next time you find yourself entertaining the idea that there's something you have to acquire in order to feel secure about your future, remember what the bank is trying to tell you: "You're richer than you think!" Try it, and see what happens! God blesses you.

Applying the Strategy
"Total Detachment"

Practical Consideration:

- Have I been seeking personal security through the acquisition and accumulation of material things?

- Do I now understand that security is a spiritual knowing-feeling that can only exist when I no longer care about worldly security?

- Given the true nature of personal security, is it clear to me why spiritual enlightenment is so rare?

Personal Application:

- By practicing nonattachment to anything that comes into my life, I am not only free to fully enjoy its presence, but also to never experience a sense of loss in its absence.

- The experience of either inner peace or constant anxiety is the direct result of the beliefs and priorities that I choose to exercise in my everyday life.

Applying the Strategy
"Total Detachment" *(cont'd)*

• There is *nothing* that I have to acquire or achieve to experience the joy, happiness, and freedom that have been mine from the beginning. I need only to sharpen my awareness, be open to all things, *and attached to nothing.*

Pertinent Quotation:

"A contented mind is the greatest blessing a man can enjoy in this world; and if, in the present life, his happiness arises from the subduing of his desires, it will arise in the next from the gratification of them."

—Joseph Addison (1672–1719)

Part V

■ STARTING EACH DAY

Morning Commitment

The principle of the "seven P's" is well known in the business world: "Prior proper planning prevents piss-poor performance!" although the Boy Scouts perhaps say it more succinctly (and certainly more delicately) in their motto, "Be prepared." This principle is no less important if you want to have a good day, regardless of what, or who, may be on your agenda for that day. This is particularly true when you're attempting to have a more meaningful experience from all that happens in your life.

Each one of us must decide for ourselves how we're going to start our day. It's the only way that we'll have any hope of sticking to the commitment we make. Naturally, your decision will be impacted by many factors. What's important to you? What results are you getting from what you're currently doing? How serious are you about effecting change in your life? How much time are you willing to commit in the morning? There is no *one* answer to any of these questions. However, there is one thing that is unequivocal about your morning commitment: once you decide what you're prepared to do, *do it!* And, if it's not possible to do it first thing in the morning, do it at your first opportunity.

Maharishi Mahesh Yogi says, "It is most important to meditate immediately upon rising, after you have washed out your mouth, before the pressures of the day descend upon you." The fact is that the encounters you *require* in your life today will happen. The only variable is your *reaction* to them. The question is, "How prepared will you be to receive the best possible outcome from each situation?"

One way to enhance the results of each encounter in your day is to select a quiet place where you can be alone, are not likely to be disturbed, and can enter into direct communication with the God of your personal understanding. Begin by speaking to him in prayer, acknowledging each anticipated event in the day. Ask that he help you to know his will in it, and to give you the strength, power, and ability to carry it out.

Your prayers are then followed by your morning meditation. As you begin, ask him to help you to remember who you really are and to "speak" to your heart. In silence, he will respond. And although his response may not be immediately discernible to you, the message or direction you require will subsequently become clear. Trust him, and each day will be better than the day before. Your progress is assured!

One common question is, "How much time do I have to spend each morning?" Spiritual coaches will tell you that they spend from one to two hours (or more) each and every morning. It may be that ten or fifteen minutes are all that you can do at the outset. If so, fine, but commit to it, and do it each morning without fail. You can extend the time commitment as you progress. It is truly a commitment that is both voluntary and self-monitored.

The investment community uses a term called "return on investment." If investment capital is a metaphor for the hours in a day, we each have twenty-four units of capital available for investment purposes. If we were to invest just one of those hours, first thing in the morning, toward preparing ourselves to get the maximum benefit out of the remaining twenty-three hours, our return on invested capital would be *exponential!* It's an investment well worth making.

Prayer

If the God of your understanding is truly engaged in representing your best interests, he is present not only during your morning prayers, but all of the time. This allows you to be in constant communication with him throughout the day and night. In fact, he is a devotee of the principle of "division of labor" and is best able to perform his duties, and to help you with yours, if there is regular feedback from you as the day progresses.

As your attention becomes focused on the magnitude of his grace and kindness, he's open to hearing a prayer of *adoration*. It helps him to know that you appreciate his compassion. This type of prayer reinforces your understanding of his considerable attributes. And truthfully, it's more important for you to express your understanding than it is for him to be adored. He's teaching you, and knows you're getting it when you acknowledge an insight.

You will also become aware of how you fell

short in some aspect of what you had planned to do, or how you "lost it" in a confrontation with someone. When this happens, he wants to hear your prayer of *contrition*. It's through acknowledging your shortcomings that you demonstrate knowledge of the right thing to do, even though you screwed up. Because if he doesn't know that you know, you'll have to repeat the lesson. It is instructive to remember what one is taught in Zen Buddhism: "To know, and not to do, is not yet to know!"

With God in your life, walking beside you each and every minute of each and every day, you will notice that you have many opportunities for prayers of *thanksgiving* for the wonderful things that he does for you. These prayers are his favorites. They show him your heart is filled with gratitude and thankfulness for the blessings you have received. And since he is always interested in your happiness, and you have told him exactly what pleases you, you can expect even more of these blessings. He may be God, but he still wants your feedback!

Last, he wants to hear your prayers of *supplication*. He waits like an anxious lover, ready to supply your every need. Tell him what you want and why you want it. Let him be the arbiter of its usefulness in helping you to awaken to the joy, happiness, and freedom you seek. Only he knows the *true* value of everything you *think* you need. Eventually, as you grow in your awareness of who you really are, your prayers of supplication will narrow to praying only to know God's will for you, and to have the strength, power, and ability to carry it out. His will for you includes that you live each moment of your life in the joy and peace of your inheritance. *Is there anything else that you want?*

Meditation

Meditation is perhaps the highest form of communication with God. Its primary purpose is to allow him to give you the guidance you seek *directly*, in the only "language" he knows—*silence*! Therefore, it is essential for you to quell the "chatter" going on in your head so his guidance can be "heard."

While there are many meditative techniques available to help you improve your communication skills, it is more important to *begin* the practice than it is to find the best technique. You can begin by simply sitting comfortably, either in a chair or cross-legged on the floor, and placing your hands together in your lap. Close your eyes and consciously relax your body from your head down to your toes, feeling the muscles slacken as you give attention to each part of your body. Then, in this relaxed condition, ask God to help you to remember who you really are, and to "speak" to your heart.

Sit quietly, allowing all thoughts to clear

from your mind. They may insist on coming back, but don't fight them. As each thought comes into your mind, simply let it go. Don't focus on it; just release it, and let it go. It can be helpful if you focus on the quiet rhythm of your breathing. Allow it to slow down and become shallower with each breath, until you feel that you're hardly breathing at all. Both your breathing and your heartbeat slow considerably during meditation.

Then, introduce a word-sound (mantra), such as the popular Sanskrit word "OM," into your awareness. The word-sound itself has little or no meaning to distract you and helps to keep other thoughts from entering your mind. The sound that you hear in your head will be *ohmmm*, which resonates well with the brain, taking you further into the meditative process and leaving the material plane behind. You will be aware of nothing at the time, but are in what is known as "the gap," the space between consciousness and God wherein all knowledge lies and, as Deepak Chopra says, "where spiritual activity commands its own laws." It is here that God "speaks" to your heart, in silence.

As you return to the moment, you may not be aware of any great insight or revelation that you were hoping to receive. That's normal in the process. However, as you progress in the practice of meditation, you will begin to "see" things much more clearly than ever before. The greatest challenge is to stay with it. The biggest reason we don't stay with the practice of meditation is performance anxiety. Regardless, as it is the single most important thing you'll ever do, don't allow your ego to convince you that you haven't the time to meditate, or that the process is too slow, or even worse, that it's not working. "Be still and know that I am God," is an instructive biblical admonition.

It is suggested that you allow about thirty minutes for the whole process of meditation. If you find it too difficult to keep your focus for thirty minutes, do it for as long as you can, and then just a little bit longer. It will get easier as you become more practiced in the technique and personally experience more of the benefits. Some feel that they are greatly advantaged by a second meditation in the evening.

The thirteenth-century theologian, Saint Thomas Aquinas, spent years trying to know God through rational defenses of Christian doctrine. His works fill multiple volumes with his thoughts and reasoning. But once he attained conscious contact with God through the meditative process, he stopped writing. When asked why, he said that what he had been shown in meditation made everything he had ever written, "seem only as straw"!

■ Part VI

■ REAL VALUE OF THE PROGRAM

Discovering Your True Identity

One of the remarkable things you will discover when you *awaken* to who you really are is that your life will be filled with joy, happiness, and freedom. These will not be just fleeting glimpses, but the daily sustainable experience of a deep and profound knowing-feeling that you are one of God's children, and as such, you possess all of the blessings that you were endowed with in the very beginning.

If you are not fully experiencing this reality, your true identity has not yet been *uncovered*, and you are encouraged to continue in your search. The biblical admonition to "seek first the kingdom of God . . . and all these things shall be added to you" (Matthew 6:33) was not an idle promise. It has been fulfilled in the lives of many who have gone before you, who, just like you and me, had no idea that such feelings of joy, happiness, and freedom were even possible, let alone available to them.

I'm reminded of the story of the search for

the missing Maltese falcon statue, which was made of pure gold. Apparently the person who stole the falcon covered it with ordinary clay so that it could be smuggled out of the country undetected. The scheme unraveled, however, when the statue was accidentally banged against another object and a chip of the clay came free, revealing the solid gold Maltese falcon beneath.

This story strikes me as a perfect metaphor for our experience in this world. We would like to think that we're more valuable, but are unable to appreciate who we really are because, over the years, we've covered our "golden reality" with so much "clay." On occasion we may have had a glimpse of our true identity when we brushed up against something and exposed a small piece of the "gold." For just a brief moment, we experienced a sense of joy, happiness, and freedom like nothing we had felt before. We were convinced at that moment that there really was a God and that all was right with the world! However, it didn't last, as the spot was quickly covered over with more "clay," and we once again lost sight of our true identity.

Our task is to unravel the scheme by discovering our true identity once and for all. Because, when we find out who we really are, we'll find the *sustainable* joy, happiness, and freedom that we've been looking for!

What We Really Are Is Perfect!

How we tend to perceive and express ourselves in this world . . . *is not!* But the good news is we can make significant improvements while we're here. In fact, that's why we're here! If we were experiencing our true perfection, as God made us, we would have no further reason to be here, and would leave our human form, allowing it to return to the Source.

The only reason we're in this world, as we perceive it, is because we had an idea that we could live our lives through *our own knowledge,* without the need of God. His response was, "Good luck!" And that was simply because he gave us the *free will* to decide whether to do it *our* way or *his* way. That is the only decision we are required to make. Anything that follows from that one decision is totally predictable.

However, being a loving father, he did not abandon us without the possibility of return. Instead, he gave us the Holy Spirit to watch over us and to act as our guide through the journey of remembering who we really are. Just exactly when that happens is up to each individual, dependent only upon how long we want to rely on our own knowledge. There's no time limit—we're free to choose.

Each time we are confronted with a new challenge in terms

of disappointment or sorrow, we're allowed to use the situation as a learning experience and to *change our minds* about how we wish to proceed. If we do *not* make a change, it will be necessary for the opportunity to be presented again, and again, and again, until we do indeed learn the lesson it was meant to teach. Then, the moment we *do* learn and make a corrective decision, there will be no need to repeat the experience. Simple, isn't it? Try it, and see what happens! God blesses you.

Opening Unseen Doors

Having allowed God into your life, you'll soon realize that he goes before you and prepares the way, and that he can open "doors" you don't even know are there. When you undertake a mission with God, all he asks is that you believe in his capabilities; go right to the end of your vision and be willing to take the next step in faith. He'll take it from there!

Most of us used to see a huge wall ahead and complain that there was no way to proceed, as the wall was too high! No matter how much we prayed to have a door appear so we could pass through, nothing happened. What we failed to realize was that God saw no reason to provide us with a door (let alone to open it) as we were nowhere near the wall. We were looking at the problem from a distance. As we weren't at the wall, why would we need a door? We weren't ready to pass through: we were just *thinking* about it. We still had a distance to go. We needed to go right up to the wall before there was any need for a door!

You will recall the allegorical story of Moses, in which he was leading the children of Israel in their exodus from Egypt ahead of the pursuing army of the Pharaoh. He sent scouts ahead to find a way out, but they returned with the bad news of a huge sea blocking their way. They said there was no choice but to turn around, go back, and try to find another way. However, this was not a viable option, as to do so would have meant certain death to all at the hands of the Pharaoh's army.

Moses insisted that God had promised to deliver them, and would do so, if they trusted him and went forward in faith, so they did. And just as soon as Moses and his people arrived at the water's edge, the sea parted—not a moment before. Why would the sea need to part if Moses and his people were not yet there? God is funny that way. He seems to insist that he will open doors only for those who have gone right up to the wall, those who are confident that a door will be there and will be opened for them. The others don't need a door!

If you have defined your God with this capability and are willing to go forward in faith, your path will be made clear or a "door" will open that you didn't even know was there. What a wonderful thing to know as you begin each new day.

What Makes Things Happen?

Your *desire and intention* to have it happen. And whether those are conscious or unconscious doesn't matter. All that's required in making anything happen is that you desire it and intend that it happens, and it will! Sounds great *spiritually* . . . but how can you know that will work in your everyday life? Can you demonstrate the principle? Absolutely, beyond any *reasonable* doubt (the kind of doubt we're most unfamiliar with).

Put your left hand out in front of you. Humor me; put out your left hand (and yes, it's okay if you use your right hand instead). Now wiggle your fingers one at a time, starting with your thumb and working your way through to the little finger (there should be five of them). Then do it again, starting with your little finger and working your way back to the thumb (should still be five of them). Who said that the search for enlightenment isn't fun?

Now, tell me how you did that. What commands did you give, and to whom? What specific process did you use to have your fingers respond exactly as you *intended* them to? None . . . you simply *intended* that they do what you *desired*, and they did it! Remarkable, isn't it? And it happened in a nanosecond. And, it's the same process used for *everything else* that happens in your life. Wow! And you thought you made everything happen. Well, actually you do, by having a desire for it, and intending that it happen. The rest is easy!

Take a few minutes and reflect on this process. It's very important to understanding, monitoring, and correcting *all* that comes into your life. You're personally in charge of any, and all, of the joy, happiness, and freedom that you experience. It simply depends on what *thoughts* you choose to entertain, and the *desire and intention* that you give to them. Talk about having control! Try it, and see what happens! God blesses you.

Standing on a Rock

O nce you have discovered who you really are, you'll be overwhelmed by a tremendous sense of *gratitude!* It will be for the joy, happiness, and freedom that are in your daily life, and for the knowledge that, in knowing who you are, you also know, by extension, who everybody else is!

You have become aware that most people (just like you and me) think that their lives are separate and apart from all others, and that each one of them (just like you and me) has constructed a history about their respective lives and experiences that they hold to be true. They will not only insist that this is who they are, but will protect the image even in the face of evidence to the contrary. It's as though their responses to life have been placed on "automatic pilot," to reflect *prior* navigational experience without recognizing the *present* reality.

It's what is known as our "ego-self" or "first voice" in spiritual dialogue. Actually, it's only our *conditioned mind's* first response to anything we encounter, and it's based on all that has gone before. It is the sum total of each past decision made to rationalize both the experience and our chosen response to it. It's all the "stuff" from which we have built both our personal identity and our so-called reality. And we're stuck with it until we find out who we *really* are!

We now understand why people hold the positions and beliefs that they do. It's their "reality story." And, it's a story that they're more than happy to defend against anybody else's "reality story." It can fuel some pretty serious arguments, particularly over who's *right* and who's *wrong*. Isn't it comforting to know that one is neither right nor wrong? It's just their conditioned response commenting on the event as they perceive it from their personal perspective. However, the facts of any situation are just the facts of the situation. Every individual is free to respond to them in whatever way they feel is appropriate to accommodate their belief system—and they do!

Knowing that you're now trying to meet life with your "second voice" further extends your gratitude. This is the one that's heard only if you've allowed your first voice to be "neutered," preventing it from "jumping" all over whatever you're confronted with. This second voice is your "spiritual self," which is not motivated by your past experience, but rather by the newfound awareness of your spiritual reality and intuitive understanding of the *present* moment.

The difference in approach by these two voices is remarkable, not only in content and direction, but also in the comfort and authority with which your second voice speaks. This is the voice that is being inspired by the Source of all knowledge who knows precisely what needs to be done or said to best position you for what is next required to happen in your life. You're definitely going to have a better day using your second voice.

Your feelings of gratitude and confidence are further enhanced each day because you have asked your God to help you to know what to do, and to give you the strength, power, and ability to carry it out in each and every encounter. You also know he goes before you and prepares the way, opening "doors" you don't even know are there. When these confidences are added to your knowledge that the Power behind you is far greater than the task ahead, your whole attitude and demeanor become positive, and good things happen to you. Is it any wonder that you feel as though you're *standing on a rock*?

The Deconstruction of the Ego

The "ego" is the *belief system* we've constructed through our personal experiences in life. It's our *conditioned mind*, and we rely on it to guide us in all that we think or do. And we insist that what it's telling us is true. At least it's *our* truth, and we'll defend it vigorously against competing "truths" preferred by others!

Of course we will. They're *our beliefs*; we made them, so naturally we'll defend them. We *believe* in them! The trouble is, they're wrong! Wow! Is that a problem or what? As Stan Laurel would say to Oliver Hardy, "It certainly is, Ollie!" Which raises the question, "How do we fix it?"

In most 12-step programs we're told that it's through ego deflation—*at depth!* In the Christian tradition it's through being born again *in the Spirit.* In Buddhism it's through achieving *enlightenment.* In each of these teachings, the ego (our entire thought system, no less) is to be "deconstructed" in favor of being guided by Spiritual Truth. Oh, is that all? Gee whiz, and I thought it might be difficult!

It would indeed be difficult, if not impossible, if we were to try to accomplish this on our own, which is to say we'll rely on our conditioned mind to guide us in the task of deflating our *ego*! This is not going to happen because *they're both the same*. We can't deflate the ego at the same level as the ego operates. That's why our efforts to do so have failed in the past. This is known as listening to our first voice. This, in spiritual dialogue, is the voice that always speaks first. It tells you what your *conditioned mind* believes—and is always wrong!

The good news, as we're told in spiritual instruction, is that the Holy Spirit has been given to each one of us to act as our guide in returning us to living in the fullness of joy, happiness, and freedom, gifts that God endowed us with in the very beginning. He speaks to us in what is known as our second voice. This is the one that is directed by the Holy Spirit, *who speaks for God* and is always right! To "hear" our second voice, we must "still" our first voice (read: not respond with our first thought) and listen carefully (read: with an *open mind*) to what the Holy Spirit moves us to either say or do.

So rather than struggle to deflate your ego, let the Holy Spirit help your mind to *reinterpret its misperceptions*. Try it, and see what happens! God blesses you.

Spiritual Vision

Rose-colored glasses have *nothing* on "spiritual vision." All that rose-colored glasses do is *tint* what you're looking at with a rosy hue, making the image appear more pleasant to the eye. "Spiritual vision" can dramatically change your perception of an event or completely remove an unacceptable image from your conscious awareness. This phenomenon is just one of the blessings you will receive as a direct result of your newfound spiritual awakening.

I'd like to share a personal example of "spiritual vision" that I experienced in my early thirties. I was struggling with what can best be described as an increasing reliance on alcohol in my search for "happiness." When I finally turned the whole matter over to God and discovered a joy and happiness far greater than I was ever able to achieve through the use of alcohol, I quit drinking altogether. However, as important as that event was, and is, in my life, it only serves as the *backdrop* to the "spiritual vision" part of the story.

What I discovered, much to my surprise and delight, was that I no longer needed to use alcohol to enjoy my life. In fact, it had been "removed" from my conscious awareness! Unless someone drew my attention to it by spilling a drink or searching for a coaster, I was not consciously aware of the presence of alcohol—it had disappeared from my "sight." And it's been that way for all these many years.

The same thing is true for smoking. I smoked for over twenty years, and after many unsuccessful attempts to quit on my own, I finally asked God to help me. He did, and I haven't smoked since. And, just like alcohol, smoking was *removed* from my sight! It's only if somebody is fussing over an ashtray or fumbling for a match that my attention is caught. Otherwise, I'm completely unaware of it. Talk about miracles!

You'll also notice that you "see" far fewer disappointments once you're allowing God to lead the way. That's mainly the result of being less inclined to set *expectations* for outcomes for which you are not responsible. Your responsibility is for *inputs*, not *outcomes*. Therefore, if you're anticipating a certain result from a planned event and it turns out differently, your attitude of "outcome acceptance" will automatically surface, negating the potential for disappointment. This allows you to still have a great day, even though your agenda has been overtaken by events *beyond* your immediate control. In fact, if you're anything like me, you'll probably find it somewhat *exciting* to watch what it is that comes into your life as a result of the revised agenda. Trust God, and watch what happens!

Your observations will also change through *seeing* many other things differently than you did before. "Spiritual vision" looks only upon "life" in all that it beholds. Whether it's the budding of a flower in spring or a funeral procession, the "good" is always recognized over the "bad" and the "ugly." And the "death" of anything is *seen* simply as an end to its present form and a return to the Source.

Experience with this phenomenon goes far beyond these examples. However, I believe that they serve to demonstrate how "spiritual vision" can change what you "see" in your life. As your spiritual reality is further uncovered, you'll experience an increasing number of similar transformations, and recognize the incredible power that's working in your best interest, as God leads the way!

When the Student Is Ready, the Teacher Will Appear

And, if you're not "ready," you don't need one! Who's in charge here? You are. So, if you'd like to create a different result in your life, don't seek out a *teacher*—get yourself ready. *Then* the teacher will appear. It's axiomatic—just as soon as one part happens, so does the other.

The missing piece of this puzzle is the knowledge of what you want in your life. Have you really thought it through? Looked at your past performances and the results they produced? Made a decision to change your behavior in whatever way necessary to achieve a different result? Adopted a willingness to change? Opened your mind to accepting a new program of action? If so, congratulations! You have recognized that changes in your life are entirely up to you, and you have made yourself ready for the teacher to appear.

So who's the teacher? How will the teacher know where to find you and that you're ready to accept a change in your life? The teacher won't. *You will.* And that is all that's required for the teacher to appear. Indeed, the teacher may not even know what you've decided to do, let alone how he or she is going to instruct you. It's not required that the teacher knows;

it is only required that you make yourself *ready*; the rest will follow automatically, and you'll then realize that they were precisely the teachers you needed, when you needed them, and where you needed them!

The message conveyed in this discussion is to spend no time at all on finding the "right" teachers, as you would have no way of evaluating their skills or expertise in any event. Spend your time and focus on getting "ready." For, as the Buddhist proverb says, "When the student is ready, the teacher will appear!" Try it, and see what happens! God blesses you.

Part VII
SHARED EXPERIENCES

Poetic Progression

Over the past many years, one of the things I've enjoyed doing is sitting down during a quiet moment and writing something. For me, this activity generally took place around the Christmas holidays, after I had wrapped up my business for the current year and was taking some personal time with my family.

During these reflective times, I would review the accomplishments of the past year and contemplate what the next year might bring. Invariably my thoughts would turn to gratitude for the many blessings that I was enjoying, not only in my business and with my wife and family, but also in the continued *unfolding* of my awareness as to the *meaning* of life.

Religious teachings offer the names of several people credited with having experienced their "spiritual awakening" through what is described as a moment of "intense light." These include the conversion of Paul on the road to Damascus and a "burning bush" in the case of Moses on Mount Sinai. In that holy instant, God *revealed* himself to them, and their lives were changed completely and forever. That was *not* what happened to me. My spiritual awakening was what is commonly referred to as the "educational variety." This type of awakening is the result of an extended series of learning experiences and more modest revelations that I subsequently recognized had entered, and altered, my awareness.

This gradual enlightenment is reflected in my writings over the last thirty years, some of which I have included here, as I believe they are germane to our discussion. The time period covered by these writings is 1976 through 1983. That's when I first recognized that significant progress was being made in my spiritual awareness.

The first of the writings, "If You're Talking to Me," is a 1976 poem describing my willingness to "hear" from God, so that I too would be a "lover that's heard." Then in 1978 I found myself writing about my "Gifts to God," which represents a rather clear demonstration of turning my will and my life over to the care of God *as I understood him.* At the same time I wrote "Thy Kingdom Come," capturing the wonderful feeling of my awareness that the Lord's Prayer had been answered in my life. Then, in 1983, the whole process of returning to God was made clear to me in the metaphorical "Come and Be a Christmas Tree." Thank you, God!

IF YOU'RE TALKING TO ME

They say that you love me, and I believe that it's so.
But if you don't tell me, then how will I know?
I know you could tell me, without speaking a word.
Then I too would be a lover that's heard.

If you're talking to me, I can't hear you.
Please say it out loud, though I'm near you.
For I want to see all the beauty in thee,
And lose any reason to fear you.

You told others you loved them, then set them free.
Still they seem so convinced that you truly love me.
They're beautiful people, and wouldn't be lying.
If I were to hear you, it would help me keep trying.

If you're talking to me, I can't hear you.
Please say it out loud, though I'm near you.
For I want to see all the beauty in thee,
And lose any reason to fear you.

If your love has conditions, I'll follow the rules.
Your word spoken softly will furnish the tools.
To hear that you love me, would settle my grief,
And turn into knowledge, what is only belief.

If you're talking to me, I can't hear you.
Please say it out loud, though I'm near you.
For I want to see all the beauty in thee,
And lose any reason to fear you.

Not knowing the truth leaves so much in doubt.
Just one word from you, would straighten things out.
So please end my searching, and allow me to hear,
That you really do love me and will always be near.

If you're talking to me, I can't hear you.
Please say it out loud, though I'm near you.
For I want to see all the beauty in thee,
And lose any reason to fear you.

GIFTS TO GOD
(Gold, Frankincense, and Myrrh)

YOU knew the many ways I had tried to find happiness and a sense of purpose in my life. I tried to gain recognition through success in business, security through the gathering of possessions, and peace of mind through the avoidance of conflict.

YOU also knew that these individual pursuits would work against the accomplishment of my objectives. Yet you allowed me to continue, for as long as I could, so that I too would know.

YOUR blessing of awareness has changed me. I now enjoy the fruits of your grace, without the need to give up or to deny myself anything. I let all things happen in your perfect order, which has always been, and always will be, in my best interest. I know who I am, where I came from, and where I'm going. I stand on a rock, comfortable in the presence of all others and confident in the knowledge that I belong. I am free from fear and apprehension, and filled with faith and trust in your divine purpose. There truly is life eternal. You gave me all of this and more, and more, and more each day, when I came to you sincerely and humbly offered my gifts of gold, frankincense, and myrrh:

Gold: I gave you all of my possessions. Everything that I owned, had use of, or came into contact with, I gave over to you, to do with according to your will. My money, house, business, talents, family, and best friends I recognize as belonging to you. You ask only that I do the best I can with each one of them.

Frankincense: I dedicated my life to you and to your purpose. My morning prayer is only to know your will for me and to have the strength, power, and ability to carry it out. You have always gone before me to prepare the way. You ask only that I follow with faith and trust.

Myrrh: I gave to you, and you alone, the right to judge the motives and results for actions taken by my fellow man, no matter how adverse the consequences may appear. You have shown me that forgiveness and compassion immediately follow the recognition of truth. You ask only that I try.

Reflection

"The fruit of the Spirit is in all goodness, righteousness, and truth" (Ephesians 5:9). What fruit are you enjoying? Are you comfortable with your life? Are you truly happy each and every day, no matter what the circumstances? Do you have peace of mind and a sense of belonging? Are you confident in all situations, free of fear and apprehension? Are you filled with faith and trust in a divine purpose? Do you know that you have eternal life? If you have all of these things, continue to do what you're doing. If you do not enjoy every one of these blessings, then change what you're doing.

You don't have to wait for Christmas to offer your gifts of gold, frankincense, and myrrh to God, as you understand him. *Unless you want to!*

THY KINGDOM COME

Creator of all things, your presence is everywhere,
  and awareness of you brings fulfillment.

When I came to know you, and the reality
  of my own existence,

My actions, here on earth, freely followed your will,
  as all in Heaven do.

Since finding your Kingdom, you've provided
  all of my needs, and I know that you always will.

I no longer sit in judgment of my fellow man,
  as I know that his actions are part of your plan.

This same knowledge has removed my feelings
  of guilt, resentment, and remorse.

Being at one with you, in your Kingdom, I am
  not led into temptation, and

Evil has no place in the lives of people
  touched by your Holy Spirit.

For you are the Power and the Glory
  that created all things for good.

It has always been this way, it is this way now,
  it will always be this way.

I am so grateful to know that I am part of you
  and your Kingdom, forever and ever. Amen.

COME AND BE A CHRISTMAS TREE

Winter is cold and so unforgiving,
When you are a tree in wilderness living.
A spectator of life from season to season,
You can't but wonder if there's really a reason.

If you only knew what you're meant to be,
A reflection of Christ as a Christmas Tree.
So come forward now and be born anew,
Be freed from the roots that are binding you.

Come live in his house with his full protection,
Enjoying the warmth of love and affection.
Then you'll be changed from imperfect and scorned,
To a vision of beauty so fully adorned.

Your branches will be laden with gifts undeserving,
A new sense of purpose from him you are serving.
These gifts you will share so freely with others,
For all will be treated as sisters and brothers.

Keeping nothing for self means everything gained,
An abundance of joy and fulfillment sustained.
There's no greater goal, no greater reward,
Than performing your mission as set by the Lord.

If you only knew what you're meant to be,
A reflection of Christ as a Christmas Tree.
So come forward now and be born anew,
Be freed from the roots that are binding you.

Be what you were meant to be.
Come and be a Christmas Tree!

Coach's Closing Comments

The existence of God does not depend on your *belief* in him. But the fullness of your joy, happiness, and freedom during your time in this world does!

Your search for your own reality will lead you to know that God created you and loves you, and that he protects your *reality* in eternity. When your body finishes the work you have assigned to it, you will leave it behind and continue as your "Original Self," joining with all others in "Spiritual Oneness." So fear not! Your "life," after the physical "death" of your body, is *not* in jeopardy. It never was, and it never will be. It's God's promise to his beloved child. Count on it!

The question is, "What do you want to happen while you're here?" You have been given the freedom to choose. Your "spiritual self" was created with the fullness of joy, happiness, and freedom from the very beginning, which is yours to enjoy if you *choose* "life." A decision for "life" means that you wish to participate in all of the blessings that are your inheritance as a child of God, right *here* and right *now!* This decision allows you the opportunity to enjoy what is generally referred to as "Heaven on earth" in the Judeo-Christian lexicon, "enlightenment" and "nirvana" in Buddhism. You'll enjoy the bliss of living a joyous, happy, and free life with childlike enthusiasm, each and every day in perpetual wonder of who you really are!

Or you can choose to live as a *self-reliant* individual, intent on controlling what happens in your life and seeking to establish special relationships with people who will bring comfort to you and meaning to your existence. With this choice comes not only the responsibility for scripting your own life and engineering acceptable outcomes, but also for judging the intentions and activities of everybody else as they relate to you and your chosen agenda. First, you are faced with this awesome task—and then you die!

The real tragedy of the second choice is not the "and then you die" part, since when you do, you'll be with God in all of your glory. It's that you'll forfeit all of the *real* joy of life that is available to you, each and every minute of each and every day while you're here!

Two things are certain. One, you *don't* have to die to be in "Heaven." And two, you *do* have to die to be in "Heaven." It just depends on the choice you make *here* and *now!* God blesses you.

Glossary

If we're to have a fruitful conversation on any subject, we should first define our terms. This is even more important if our topic is at all controversial or subject in large part to one's own belief system and personal experiences. The following are some of the terms used throughout the book that I believe require definition.

Ego-self: Our false "reality," created through "separation" from God, to conduct our affairs in ignorance of his will for us; a substitute for the "spiritual self" that God created; a thought system that gives rise to sin, guilt, and fear; the "protector" of our separated individuality; the powerful, personal, motivating force with no plan for success, only a never-ending drive for "more" to try to satisfy our feelings of need.

God: The Prime Source of all being and life; the one known as "Father," whose fatherhood was established through his "First Cause," creating his son, the "Effect" known as "the Christ"; the one whose essence is pure spirit, permeating all creation; whose unity is the *state* of Heaven; and the one who is described simply as, "I am," for to add anything else to the statement would be to limit, by definition, that which is *without* limit.

Note: To avoid issues of religious sensitivity (see "God, Religion, and Gender" on page 8), in the hope of keeping our focus on universal spiritual themes, I've used the word God throughout the book to represent most facets of that which is divine. Some readers might be more comfortable substituting the descriptive language of their personal religious beliefs.

Heaven: The preseparation world of God and his unified creation, *exclusive* of the world of perception; the perfect union of God's will and spirit; a state that can be reflected in the *here and now,* through a holy relationship with the *real* world; the peaceful knowing-feeling that God is in his Heaven and all is "right" with the world.

Holy Spirit: The communication *link* between God and us as his "separated" sons, allowing us to share the totality of his love; bridging the gap between the mind of Christ and our "split minds" (duality of spirit and separation); the one who leads us through our *illusions* to the truth; the "voice" of God, who speaks for him and for our spiritual selves, reminding us of our *true* identities we had forgotten.

Son of God: The *totality* of the Sonship of God; the "Effect" of the "First Cause"; the "Self" that God created by the extension of his spirit; known as "the Christ" who is our *true* self; an *expression* of our unified relationship to God. It is the Son's function in Heaven to create, as it was God's in creating him.

Spiritual Awakening: Waking from the "dream" of separation to the *reality* of who we really are; knowing that we live in the *here and now*, in *eternity*, as an integral part of the oneness we share in Christ; exceptionally aware of the joy, happiness, and freedom that is ours and has been from the beginning; recognizing that the Holy Spirit goes before us and prepares the way; and communicating with the world through our spiritual reality.

Spiritual Self: The *changeless* and *eternal* spiritual nature of our true reality in contrast to the ego-self, personified in our body, which *changes* and *dies*; the thought in God's mind, which is the unified Christ; our reality as *pure spirit* in the *image* of God, our Father.

Membership and Program Support

Membership in the Spiritual Coach Program is simply a matter of registering at our website www.thespiritualcoach.net. Select the "Electronic Outreach" page from the menu, fill in the contact information on the form provided, and press "Send." Membership is free.

As a registered member you will receive an e-mail every week to share in the Coach's Weekly Message. Members are also entitled to submit questions about the program by e-mail directly to the coach. (Only registered members may submit questions.)

Financial Support for the Program

The Spiritual Coach Program relies entirely on the royalties from book sales and the income generated from speaking engagements, seminars, and retreats to cover all operating costs and program development expenses. If you would like to engage the coach to participate in a forthcoming event, please contact us directly at coach@thespiritualcoach.net.

Index

About the Author

S tan Sanderson is the founder of The Spiritual Coach and creator of the Spiritual Coach Program. He studied the technique of Transcendental Meditation in the early 1970s, as taught by His Holiness Maharishi Mahesh Yogi through the International Meditation Society. His personal spiritual experiences were confirmed in *A Course in Miracles*, which he has fully embraced and which also helped inform his universal spiritual principles.

Over many years, Stan has used his personal experience and teaching skills to help others find the happiness they seek. He recently set up a website, www.thespiritualcoach.net, to provide an "electronic outreach" for members of the Spiritual Coach Program.

Stan enjoyed successful careers in both the medical supply business and the financial services industry before retiring from active business in 2001. He has been an industry leader, having served as both president and chairman of the board of directors for the Canadian Association of Financial Planners (CAFP) and president of the Canadian Surgical Trade Association (CSTA).

His public service commitments have included accepting an appointment by the government of Ontario to serve as a trustee and, subsequently, as chairman of the board of trustees for the Ontario Public Service Employees Union Pension Plan. His biography is listed in the Canadian Who's Who.

Stan is married with four children and eight grandchildren. He and his wife, Elizabeth, recently moved from their family home in Oakville to the Villages of Leacock Point in Orillia, Ontario.